RAF · FRONTLINE

The Royal Air Force – Defending the Realm

**Photography by
John M. Dibbs**

Text – Tony Holmes / Jon Lake

Airlife

England

RAF · FRONTLINE

The Royal Air Force – Defending the Realm

First published in the UK in 1998 by Airlife Publishing Ltd

British Library Cataloguing-in-Publication Data
A catalogue record for this book is available from the British Library

ISBN 1 85310 834 7

Photographs ©1998 John M. Dibbs
Text ©1998 Tony Holmes and Jon Lake
Designed by Karen Baker
Printed in Italy

Acknowledgements
Tony Holmes and John Dibbs wish to thank the following individuals for their help in supplying the quotes used in this volume:
Flt Lt Andy Thomas Sentry Standards Unit, RAF Waddington. *Sqn Ldr Kev Mason* No 8 Sqn, RAF Waddington.
Sqn Ldrs Dave Fry and Dave Gunn No 70 Sqn, RAF Lyneham. *Flt Andy Shenton and Flt Sgt Simon 'OB' O'Brien* No 33 Sqn, RAF Benson.
Flt Lt Gary Weightman No 101 Sqn, RAF Brize Norton. *Flt Lt 'Windy' Miller* 'B' Flight No 22 Sqn, RAF Wattisham.
Sqn Ldr Jon Hancock Headquarters Allied Forces North Europe. *Sqn Ldr Rob Lea* No 20 (R) Sqn, RAF Wittering. *Flt Lt Bill Auckland* No 19 (R) Sqn, RAF Valley.
Sqn Ldr Phil Flint RAF Valley. *Flt Lt Andy Gent* formerly No 19 (R) Sqn, RAF Valley. *Flt Lt Steve Grant* No 19 (R) Sqn, RAF Valley.
Flt Lt Chris Hadlow No 19 (R) Sqn, RAF Valley. *Flt Lt Nige Ingle* No 208 (R) Sqn, RAF Valley. *Wg Cdr Ray Lock* Chief Instructor, RAF Valley.
Flt Lt James Morris No 19 (R) Sqn, RAF Valley. *Sqn Ldr Gordon Robertson* No 12 Sqn, RAF Lossiemouth.
Flt Lt Andy Cubin Red Arrows, RAF Cranwell/Scampton. *Flt Lt Clair Hansell* Community Relations Officer, RAF Benson.
Sqn Ldr Ted Querzani/Sqn Ldr Christopher Bartle Community Relations Officer, RAF Lyneham. *Flt Lt Dave Rowe* Community Relations Officer, RAF Brize Norton.

Sqn Ldr Kevin Mason 8 Sqn. *Flt Lt Chris Hadlow* 6 Sqn. *Sqn Ldr Al Thoroughgood* 11 Sqn. *Flt Lt Pete Hackett* 25 Sqn. *Flt Lt John Sheilds* 25 Sqn. *Sqn Ldr Kelvin Truss* 5 Sqn.
Sqn Ldr Bruce Graeme-Cook 16 Sqn. *Sqn Ldr Chris Huckstep* 1 Sqn.

Cameraship pilots:
Flt Lt Andy Gent 19 Sqn. *Flt Lt Spike Jepson. Flt Lt Simon Tickle. Flt Lt Bill Auckland. Sqn Ldr Neil Benson. Flt Lt 'Foo' Kennard. Sqn Ldr Mike Johnson.*
Flt Lt Steve Noujaim. Alan Walker.
Special thanks to:
Air Commodore Gordon McRobbie. Wing Commander John Teager. Wing Commander John Scholtens.
RAF Strike Command Public Relations Office – *Chris Shepherd.*
Personnel & Training Command Public Relations Office – *John Turner. Sqn Ldr Andy Wyatt.*
The Commanding Officers & personnel at RAF Valley – *Sqn Ldr Neil Benson. Flt Lt Andy Gent* (formerly 19 Sqn, RAF Valley.) *Flt Lt Steve Noujaim* (100 Sqn, RAF Leeming.)

Airlife Publishing Ltd
101 Longden Road, Shrewsbury, SY3 9EB, England

Contents

Author's Note

The world of the military aviator is exceptional. Imagine throwing 20 tonnes of hardware down a jagged valley at speeds in excess of 500 mph – hurling your machine as close as possible to the clawing granite in order to evade detection. That is about as exciting an occupation as you or I can conceive. Now change that scenario to a pack of four jets being hunted down by an invisible 'enemy' and make it rain *hard*, during the pitch-black of night, and it becomes a place we probably don't even want to imagine. Elsewhere, far out in the Atlantic you may find a solitary yellow helicopter battling in similar conditions to extract the beleaguered crew of a sinking vessel that has been battered by the merciless seas. The television news brings you images of a Hercules delivering urgent supplies to starving refugees in an 'area of tension'. This is the world of the Frontline pilots and crews in the Royal Air Force during the late 1990s. Training and attitude are key. At the end of the day it's a simple equation – you can either do it or you're not allowed to do it. There is no halfway house.

I have witnessed this elite force in action during the compilation of this book – a photographic study of the UK-based defence assets. With it, I hope to convey the ability of the pilots and groundcrew of today's RAF. The dedicated men and women of the service are assembled to propel the aforementioned piece of hardware down that valley, or to locate that boat. Each is ultimately responsible for a safe return – professionalism is only part of it. However, these are not easy times for our RAF, the 'kit' is getting old and the budgets are being cut, but a world-class force is what is required and the personnel do their utmost to deliver. After all, there are no points for second place.

As we approach the new millennium, the fast jet in many ways defines the achievement of man. Technologically sophisticated with phenomenal speed and power, it has the ability to penetrate the deep blue seemingly without regard for Isaac Newton or his theories. So glamorous and exciting to the bystander, what you miss out on is Sir Isaac's revenge – the crushing '*g*' force working on the occupants once a radar warning receiver 'alerts' the crew of unwanted company. The vortices, ripping off the tips of the wings, eat your aircraft's precious energy. The ground rolls round your field of view, rushing up to meet you whilst the airframe judders and the engines are applied at maximum power. Blinking the stinging sweat out of your eyes, you strain for visual contract, hoping that the other pilot – he or she – doesn't want to follow you.

It's a challenging and demanding work environment, with images that are never to be forgotten. Hopefully though, through the four years of photographic work that this volume represents, and the quotations from 'the sharp end' you will be able to appreciate what is being done on our behalf all over the world, so we can sit at home in safety and read this book – on a rainy, pitch-black night.

I need to thank a thousand people for the opportunity afforded to me for this project. I have met many exceptional people and wish to thank them all. In particular, I would like to thank Air Commodore Gordon McRobbie and his staff at Whitehall for the assistance and backing for this project, especially Wing Commander John Teager who was invaluable in his guidance for the content and structure. Wing Commander John Scholtens also gave greatly of his much-demanded time. Chris Shepherd at Strike Command PR and his staff unselfishly dealt with the huge amount of requests and paperwork that a project like this creates. John Turner at Personnel & Training PR was also invaluable, along with the Officers and Command of all the RAF Groups involved.

In direct regard to the flying – the images in this book could only be created if the photographer was not only airborne, but in the right place, and that right place was sometimes only a 2 ft square piece of air. It is due to the skill of the aircrew that I was able to deliver such an array of images.

I would like to show my gratitude for the skill and kindness extended by 19 Sqn RAF Valley, especially the 'Boss', Sqn Ldr Neil Benson; Flt Lt Andy Gent, whose gifted hands finally got to fly a Spitfire whilst we worked on this project, taking the 19 Sqn pilot's flying experience full circle, and Flt Lt Steve Noujaim who did likewise. Flt Lt Bill Auckland and Sgt Rick Brewell also assisted greatly.

I thank Sqn Ldr Jon 'Herbie' Hancock who had enough faith to trust me in the early days with 'his' F.3 photography and set many a ball rolling. Thanks also to Willy Hackett of 25 Sqn, Al Thorogood of 11 Sqn and the pilots of 100 Sqn RAF Leeming.

I would also like to thank Allan Burney of *Aircraft Illustrated* for his support.

The photographs created for this book were shot on Canon EOS-1N bodies, a selection of Canon and Sigma lenses, as well as Mamiya 645. The film stock used was Fuji Velvia 50ASA transparency, all carried in CCS holdalls.

Dedication: This book is dedicated to the memory of my father, John W. Dibbs, the man who subtly nurtured in me the will to create and excel in all I do.

John M. Dibbs
September 1998

LOW-LEVEL ATTACK AND STRIKE

The Tornado was designed and built as a collaborative venture between Britain, Germany and Italy, and deliveries to the partner air forces began in 1980. In RAF service, the Tornado IDS (Interdictor Strike) variant replaced the Vulcan, Canberra and Buccaneer in the overland strike, attack and reconnaissance roles. The RAF procured 229 production Tornado IDS aircraft (as the Tornado GR 1) and these equipped a peak total of eleven frontline squadrons (including two recce-tasked units), eight of them based in RAF Germany (including one reconnaissance squadron).

Although the Tornado force was reduced in size following the end of the Cold War, four squadrons in RAF Germany (Nos IX, 14, 17 and 31) remain operational in the attack role, with two more UK-based units flying GR 1As (Nos II and 13) in the reconnaissance and attack roles, two more flying GR 1Bs (Nos 12 and 617) in the joint maritime and overland roles and the Tornado OCU for training. The UK-based Tornados are described more fully in the maritime and reconnaissance sections of this book.

The RAF Germany-based Tornado units operate with a wide range of weapons. The Tornado has now lost its nuclear strike commitment, while the JP.233 airfield attack weapon is gradually fading from the scene as the medium level role steadily gains in importance, and because of the ban on mines. Nos IX and 31 Squadrons include the BAe ALARM anti-radar missile among their weapons, and can operate in a defence suppression or pathfinder role. No 14 Squadron is the RAF's primary TIALD squadron, though all of the Tornado units deployed on Operation *Jural* have TIALD-qualified crews.

The Tornado force is tightly stretched, fulfilling training commitments in the USA and Canada, and maintaining operational detachments in both Saudi Arabia for peacekeeping/monitoring operations over Southern Iraq (Operation *Jural*) and in Turkey for similar operations over Northern Iraq (Operation *Warden*). For these deployments, the basic GR 1 (and the GR 1A and GR 1B) have a limited medium level reconnaissance capability, using the Vinten 18 Series 601 GP1 pod.

Some 142 surviving IDS Tornados (including recce-capable GR 1As and maritime GR 1Bs) are being rotated through a major Mid Life Upgrade programme. This was originally defined as a radical upgrade of the Tornado and its systems, to allow covert penetration of hostile airspace and the delivery of modern, new weapons with much improved accuracy and from greater stand-off range. The scope and extent of the upgrade was subsequently reduced due to budgetary constraints, though the resulting GR 4 will still represent a colossal improvement over the GR 1.

The upgrade will see the installation of an enhanced weapons control system with a MIL STD 1553B databus and with MIL STD 1760 architecture, a new GEC TICM II fixed forward looking infra-red sensor, a new wide angle Holographic HUD (allowing standard HUD symbology to be overlaid on the FLIR image), provision for the TIALD laser designator pod, a video recorder, a pilot's Multi-Function Head Down Display (for FLIR or TIALD imagery or presentation of a new digital moving map), and GPS. A Marconi Zeus RWR will replace the existing Sky Guardian equipment.

The upgrade will also include structural work to ensure that the aircraft will be able to fully exploit its new capabilities for many years to come. The Tornados involved in the programme are first flown to RAF St Athan, where they are returned to a common agreed standard (with the removal of all temporary modifications and STFs) before going to BAe's Warton plant for the upgrade itself.

Opposite Tornado GR 1B / No 617 Sqn / 2 x CBLS / RAF Lossiemouth

BAe Harrier GR 7

The Harrier GR 7 is the latest variant of the famous Harrier 'jump jet', the world's first VTOL-capable fighter-bomber. In fact, the Harrier usually makes a more conventional rolling-vertical take-off, with a contribution from wing lift dramatically reducing fuel burn and increasing payload range capability by allowing take-offs at higher weights. This is referred to by the acronym STOVL (Short Take-Off and Vertical Landing).

For many years, the primary role of the Harrier was expected to be one of halting any advance by the massed tank armies of the Warsaw Pact if ever they rolled forward, operating from hastily-prepared forward airstrips in the countryside, or even in urban areas. With the end of the Cold War it is unlikely that the RAF Harriers will ever have to operate from German supermarket car parks or farms, but the aircraft's ability to operate from austere semi-prepared and very short strips gives it an unmatched versatility and flexibility in post Cold War peacekeeping, monitoring and out-of-area operations.

Developed jointly by BAe and McDonnell Douglas, the second-generation Harrier is a more capable and advanced aircraft than its predecessor, with a low drag, high-lift carbonfibre composite wing and advanced avionics. Today's Harrier pilot has an advanced Ferranti inertial navigation system with a moving map display, as well as an integrated defensive EW suite which includes a Marconi Zeus internal ECM system, Celsius Tech BOL chaff dispensers and a Plessey Missile Approach Warning System.

The second-generation Harrier assumed a subtly different role to that undertaken by its predecessor, with more emphasis on hitting targets further behind the frontline. This inferred operating at longer ranges, but also necessitated improved night attack capability, since enemy reinforcements were most likely to 'move up' under cover of darkness. The Harrier GR 7 thus features additional night attack capability, with an NVG compatible cockpit and a GEC Avionics FLIR mounted above the nose.

The end of the Cold War saw an increased emphasis on medium level operations, and the Harrier force have received a number of new weapons to allow effective operation in this role, including CRV.7 rockets and CBU-87 cluster bombs. Even more important is the Paveway II laser-guided bomb.

The Harrier GR 7 used LGBs for its baptism of fire over Bosnia. Participating in Operation *Deliberate Force*, the UN's pre-prepared response to the inevitable violations of humanitarian agreements, the Harriers attacked a number of targets between 30 August and 14 September and again between 8 and 10 October. The Harriers tended to operate in fours, with a Jaguar GR 1B accompanying each pair, using its TIALD pod to designate targets for the Harriers.

The Harrier is now most likely to get TIALD which would give the aircraft an autonomous, self-designation capability. The aircraft will also receive the new Brimstone anti-armour weapon and Paveway III LGBs.

The Harrier's Short Take-Off and Vertical Landing (STOVL) capabilities make it ideally suited for shipboard operations, and in 1995, the RAF formally signed an agreement to reinstate the maritime capability of its GR 7s. In early 1997 No 1 Squadron deployed operationally aboard HMS *Illustrious* as part of Operation *Ocean Wave 97*. This was not the first time RAF Harrier GR 7s have deployed aboard a Royal Navy carrier, but marks the start of a new era for joint-service Harrier operations, with RN Sea Harrier F/A2s and RAF GR 7s operating together as a Mixed Fighter Force in support of the UK's new Joint Rapid Deployment Force. The RAF aircraft bring a new level of night attack capability and ground attack/offensive support expertise to the carrier air wing.

The two Harrier GR 7 squadrons based at RAF Laarbruch in Germany, Nos 3 and IV are expected to return to the UK (to Cottesmore) during 1999, while No 1 Squadron and the conversion unit, No 20 (Reserve) Squadron will remain at nearby Wittering.

SEPECAT Jaguar GR 1A, 1B and GR 3

Every slippage in the estimated in-service date for the new Eurofighter represents a need to run on those aircraft the Eurofighter is intended to replace. Fortunately, Eurofighter delays also mean deferred spending, and the money saved in a given year can be used to modernise, upgrade and improve the aircraft which will cover the gap.

Nowhere has that money been spent more effectively than in the ongoing upgrade to the RAF's Jaguars, which serve with three frontline squadrons (Nos 6, 41 and 54) at RAF Coltishall, and with a training unit (No 16 (Reserve) Squadron) at RAF Lossiemouth. The Gulf War led to a general acknowledgement of the Jaguar's usefulness and versatility. The aircraft's easy and rapid deployability (a function of no-nonsense engineering and design, and of regular practice in support of AMF and SACEUR Strategic Reserve operations) means that a Jaguar Squadron can be deployed to a trouble-spot at a moment's notice, and can be up, running and fully operational almost as soon as it arrives. This makes it ideal for the kind of operations which have characterised the post Cold War world. Designed as a dedicated low-level ground attack aircraft, the Gulf War and operations over Bosnia have seen the aircraft operating with great success at medium altitude, using a number of newly acquired weapons and systems.

Instead of retiring in the mid-1990s (as was once planned), the aircraft has been extensively modernised for continued service until about 2009. When the RAF found that it had a critical shortage of laser-designation capability, an Urgent Operational Requirement was issued to integrate GEC's TIALD pod (Thermal Imaging Airborne Laser Designator, already in limited service with Tornado) onto another frontline fast jet. The Jaguar was chosen almost by default, but has proved to be extremely successful. Ten aircraft were modified to GR 1B standards (and two to T 2B standards) by DERA and RAF St Athan, the first of these starting operations over Bosnia within a year of the contract award. As well as TIALD, the GR 1B gained a MIL STD 1553B digital databus, a new combined TV and digital moving map display, GPS and HOTAS controls. The GR 1Bs have been used by Nos 6 and 54 Squadrons.

The rest of the Jaguar force is being upgraded to broadly similar standards by a unique partnership incorporating the DRA, Logistics Command and the frontline, which allows the RAF to act as the 'intelligent customer', producing the required modification at minimum cost and in the shortest timescale. The package of modifications is being incorporated in two stages (known as Jaguar 96 and Jaguar 97) and the eventual full-standard GR 3 will incorporate the Terprom terrain reference navigation system, a new PC-based mission planner, a new display screen, a helmet-mounted sight and ASRAAM missile compatability, as well as TIALD. All GR 3s will be compatible with TIALD and recce pods, and will equip all three frontline Jaguar units, although the recce task will remain the specialisation of No 41 Squadron. The combination of Terprom, GPS and INS have vastly improved what was already an impressive level of navigational accuracy. The helmet sight and ASRAAM will make the ponderous Jaguar arguably the RAF's most capable close-in dogfighter, with true off-boresight capability.

Other modifications may be incorporated, including DVI, FLIR, and EW improvements, and it now seems likely that the aircraft will be re-engined to improve performance. Weapons currently employed by the Jaguar force include slick and retarded 1,000 lb bombs, Paveway II laser-guided bombs, BL755 and CBU-87 cluster bombs, CRV-7 high velocity aircraft rockets and overwing AIM-9 Sidewinders for self defence. The aircraft is also fitted with a pair of internal 30-mm cannon.

Opposite SEPECAT Jaguar GR 1A / No 41 Sqn / 1,000 lb AN/ALQ-101(V), Phimat & 2 x AIM-9L / RAF Coltishall

Panavia Tornado GR 1B

The Tornado replaced the Buccaneer in the maritime strike/attack role from 1993, when the reduction in Cold War tensions allowed the disbandment of three German-based IDS units under the Options for Change defence review.

In some respects, the Tornado GR 1B is a less versatile anti-shipping aircraft than the Buccaneer, with a rather shorter radius of action, and with a more restricted choice of weapons. The primary maritime attack weapon is still the BAe Sea Eagle, which gives a formidable stand off range and genuine fire-and-forget capability. The Tornado GR 1B presently lacks the Buccaneers self-designation capability for laser-guided bombs, or for TV-guided Martel missiles, which have been retired.

The Tornado is, however, a much more effective low-level attack platform, with a superior navigation system, higher low-level speed, and a vastly superior defensive aids system. The aircraft also has a useful laser rangefinder and marked target seeker, giving great accuracy in the delivery of conventional unguided air-to-surface weapons.

Moreover, Sea Eagle is a superb anti-shipping weapon, with a Microturbo turbojet engine giving a long range, and with a huge warhead giving the missile colossal lethality. The missile flies to the target at sea-skimming height and high speed, and tactics are well-refined to result in large numbers of missiles engaging a target simultaneously, from every possible direction.

The two Lossiemouth-based squadrons spend only about 40 per cent of their time training for the maritime role, and they retain a number of vital overland commitments. The units regularly participate in Operation *Jural* – the RAF's participation in UN enforcement of the southern no fly zone over Iraq. This commitment has allowed aircrew from Nos 12 and 617 Squadrons to become fully trained in using TIALD and Paveway laser-guided bombs – systems which would be exceptionally useful to the units in attacking surface targets lying close in to the coast. Like the rest of the RAF's Tornados, the GR 1Bs will undergo

upgrade to become GR 4s. The GR 4 modification will mean that all IDS Tornados in the RAF inventory will be nominally compatible with the Sea Eagle, though the unique demands of the anti-shipping role will almost certainly dictate that part-dedicated squadrons will continue to operate with the missile.

Above Tornado GR 1 / No 15 (R) Sqn / RAF Lossiemouth

Opposite Tornado GR 1B / No 12 Sqn / 2 x Sea Eagle, Sky Shadow, BOZ-107 / RAF Lossiemouth

BAe Nimrod MR 2

The Nimrod replaced the Avro Shackleton in the maritime patrol and ASW roles from late 1969. The aircraft's four Rolls-Royce Spey turbofans allow it to transit to and from its operating area at high speed and high altitude, then descend to low-level where it can shut down two engines and operate with great economy. The aircraft subsequently underwent a major upgrade during the late 1970s, which gave the new MR 2 variant improved mission systems and armament. The aircraft carries a crew of 13 (pilot, co-pilot, flight engineer, route and tactical navigators, an Air Electronics Officer and seven AEOps) and is equipped with a Searchwater surface search radar, acoustic sensors and magnetic anomaly detection gear.

Link 11 JTIDS has been fitted to some Nimrods, most notably those used in Operation *Sharp Guard* – the operation monitoring shipping in the Adriatic, in support of UN embargoes against participants in the conflicts in the former Yugoslavia. The equipment allows friendly units to share information in real-time, via secure datalink. This allows the Nimrod, surface ships and other aircraft to share a common 'surface picture'. By night, visual identification of ships can now be made using a GEC Sandpiper IR sensor, which may be turret-mounted below the starboard wing for certain operations. Some maritime Nimrods retain a powerful searchlight in the nose of their starboard wing tank. Today, the Nimrod flies with three frontline squadrons (Nos 120, 201 and 206) from RAF Kinloss.

After a fierce competition, BAe's Nimrod 2000 was selected to replace the existing Nimrod, in response to Air Staff Requirement 420. Some 21 aircraft (of 24 remaining in service, with three more in store) will be extensively rebuilt and refurbished, with a new mission system by GEC-Marconi and Boeing, RACAL Searchwater 2000MR radar and more fuel efficient BMW-Rolls-Royce BR710-series turbofan engines. The conversion process will see 80 per cent of the Nimrod's airframe being dismantled, and 60 per cent will actually be replaced, including the entire wing, which will contain increased fuel tankage.

The wing will also be of increased area, compensating for the aircraft's 20 per cent higher take-off weight.

The Nimrod 2000 will carry the same 12,000-lb weapon-load as its predecessor, but will have four underwing pylons in addition to the internal bay. Each pylon could carry a single AGM-84 Harpoon ASM, with two Sidewinders on auxiliary lateral stub pylons. The flight deck is entirely redesigned, becoming a two-crew EFIS cockpit, displacing the flight engineer. The refitted cabin will contain seven new display consoles for the Tactical co-ordinator and the rest of the seven-man mission crew.

The first stripped Nimrod MR 2 fuselages have already been airlifted from Kinloss to Hurn for conversion. The airframes will eventually go to BAe at Warton, where they will be 'finished' off. The first MR 4 for the RAF will be delivered to Boscombe Down for evaluation in 2002, and redeliveries to Kinloss will begin later that year.

Above Nimrod MR 2 / No 201 Sqn / RAF Kinloss

Opposite Nimrod MR 2 & Tornado GR 1B / Nos 201 & 12 Sqns, RAF Kinloss & RAF Lossiemouth

LOW-LEVEL ATTACK AND STRIKE

PORTFOLIO

Above Harrier GR 7 / No 20 (R) Sqn / 1,000 lb GP & SNEB pods / RAF Wittering

Opposite Tornado GR 1B / No 617 Sqn / 4 x 1,000 lb GP, Sky Shadow & BOZ-107 / RAF Lossiemouth

'I would prefer to go into a target at low-level because I know that the Tornado GR 1 is a lousy fighter. It doesn't turn and it's got no thrust – indeed, as soon as you go above 1,000 ft all of the thrust drops off. Cruising around at 25,000 ft is fine for the Americans, whose jets are optimised for it, but for the Tornado, which is designed for low-level work, it is simply not a good place to be. If you asked RAF strike crews where they felt most happy, I'm sure that they would all say down at low-level. We have trained to fly at that altitude, and you are less likely to be hit by fighters near the ground, particularly at night.'

Sqn Ldr Ray Lock, No 9 Sqn

Above Harrier GR 7 / No 20 (R) Sqn / 2 x 1,000 lb GP / RAF Wittering

Opposite Jaguar GR 1A / No 16 (R) Sqn / 1 x 1,000 lb Paveway LGB, Phimat & AN/ALQ-101(V) / RAF Lossiemouth

Above Tornado GR 1B / No 617 Sqn / 2 x CBLS, Sky Shadow & BOZ-107 / RAF Lossiemouth

Opposite Harrier GR 7 / No 20 (R) Sqn / 4 x 1,000 lb GP / RAF Wittering

'Once you have achieved combat readiness on the squadron and you are familiar with how the Tornado handles in an offensive configuration, the big thing then is to adapt to working with your navigator so that you get what you need from him, and vice versa. Once you have achieved this as a single crew, you can then look at expanding your role by working with other jets, and therefore increasing the effectiveness of the strike package.'

Flg Off Nige Ingle, No 617 Sqn

'The front cockpit of the Harrier T 10 is almost identical to that of the GR 7, and it possesses comparable handling qualities in all but the jet-borne regime, where the T 10's performance suffers as a result of its increased weight. Needless to say, the T 10 is proving to be an excellent training aid on the OCU, where it is not only used for basic circuit training, but also for teaching air combat manoeuvring, weaponeering and low-level flying.'

Sqn Ldr Rob Lea, No 20 (R) Sqn

Above Harrier T 10 / No 20 (R) Sqn / RAF Wittering

Opposite Jaguar GR 1A / No 41 Sqn / 1,000 lb GP, AN/ALQ-101(V), Phimat & 2 x AIM-9L / RAF Coltishall

'The Jaguar really is one of the last frontline combat aircraft that can be considered a "real man's" jet. It currently has no autopilot or sophisticated flying aids, which means that you are totally "hands on" all the time – it truly is a "lump of heavy metal"! There is an old joke in our community about how the Jaguar was intended to be used as an advanced trainer when it was initially ordered – if it had served in this role it would have certainly sorted the men from the boys.'

Flt Lt Chris Hadlow, No 6 Sqn

Opposite Harrier T 10 / No 20 (R) Sqn / RAF Wittering

Right Jaguar GR 1A / No 16 (R) Sqn / 1 x 1,000 lb Paveway LGB, Phimat & AN/ALQ-101(V) / RAF Lossiemouth

'At low-level the GR 1 is hugely stable, goes reasonably fast over a fair distance and is reasonably accurate. However, its limits are the man in the back, the man in the front and its radar. In respect to the latter, if you are not getting sufficient radar returns, then without GPS, twin INAS or laser-gyros, you are not going to get the totally accurate picture achievable in jets fitted with this equipment. The TFR in the GR 1 works fine in Europe, where the topography is hugely varied, thus giving great radar returns.'

Flg Off Nige Ingle, No 617 Sqn

Above Tornado GR 1B / No 617 Sqn / 4 x 1,000 lb GP, Sky Shadow & BOZ-107 / RAF Lossiemouth

Right Tornado GR 1B / Nos 12 & 617 Sqns / 2 x Sea Eagle, 4 x 1,000 lb GP, Sky Shadow and BOZ-107 / RAF Lossiemouth

'The Jaguar did a marvellous job in the Gulf War, achieving a 97 per cent serviceability rate and suffering no losses in combat. After the cessation of hostilities it became a fight to keep the jets in their wartime configuration, as all the "good bits" added to make the Jaguar a viable combat platform were progressively removed in order to save money. A perfect illustration of this was the struggle to keep two radios in the jet, as it was deemed that we only needed one in peacetime. When you are constantly performing large-scale combined exercises you need a second radio permanently tuned to your AWACS aircraft, as your primary set will be used for inter-formation communication. This requirement has finally be addressed with the Jaguar 96/97 programme, when all jets will have two radios fitted as standard.'

Flt Lt Chris Hadlow, No 6 Sqn

Opposite Tornado GR 1B / Nos 12 & 617 Sqns / 2 x Sea Eagle, 4 x 1,000 lb GP, Sky Shadow & BOZ-107 / RAF Lossiemouth

Right Jaguar GR 1 / No 16 (R) Sqn / Phimat, AN/ALQ-101(V) & 1,000 lb Paveway LGB / RAF Lossiemouth

Above Jaguar GR 1A / No 16 (R) Sqn / Phimat, AN/ALQ-101(V) & 1 x 1,000 lb Paveway LGB / RAF Lossiemouth

Opposite Jaguar T 2A / No 16 (R) Sqn / RAF Lossiemouth

Above Tornado GR 1B / No 617 Sqn / 2 x CBLS / RAF Lossiemouth

Opposite Tornado GR 1 / TTTE / RAF Cottesmore

'Operating the Tornado in the maritime role is of course different in many respects to operating the aircraft overland. However, good crew co-ordination is the key to success in either scenario. Overland, deconfliction with other friendly jets over the target is required, and therefore timing is critical. Over the sea, again timing is critical, but in this case it is to ensure all weapons arrive at the target together, thereby swamping the defensive missile systems. An added complication to maritime operations is that the target tends to move, and locating it can be a problem. However, a Maritime Patrol Aircraft (MPA) would be expected to have located the target and to have broadcast the position. All things considered, overland is probably the more difficult role; airspace restrictions, the need for accurate navigation throughout and the greater risk of encountering other aircraft, probably tip the balance. It is certainly the more interesting, as one part of the sea tends to look very much like any other – and it is always flat.'

Sqn Ldr Gordon Robertson, No 12 Sqn

Left Jaguar GR 1A / No 16 (R) Sqn / Phimat, AN/ALQ-101(V) & 1,000 lb Paveway LGB / RAF Lossiemouth

Opposite Tornado GR 1B / No 12 Sqn / 2 x Sea Eagle, Sky Shadow & BOZ-107 / RAF Lossiemouth

'When the MPA broadcasts its "Surpic"(the Surface Picture), I will be busy noting targeting details and reprogramming the kit. The management of the tactics in the GR 1B is largely controlled from the rear seat to ensure that all aircraft have the same target details, routing and timing. On the approach to the target the MPA will pass VASTAC (Vector ASsisted TACtic) information and the navigator will silently monitor the range and bearing changes, altering the kit, if necessary, to take into account any target movement.'

Sqn Ldr Gordon Robertson, No 12 Sqn

Left Jaguar GR 1A / No 41 Sqn / Phimat & AN/ALQ-101(V), 1,000 lb HE & 2 x AIM-9L /

RAF Coltishall

Opposite Tornado GR 1B / No 617 Sqn / 2 x Sea Eagle, Sky Shadow & BOZ-107

Nimrod MR 2 / No 201 Sqn / RAF Kinloss & RAF Lossiemouth

Above Jaguar GR 1A / No 41 Sqn / 1 x 1,000 lb GP, 2 x AIM-9L, Phimat
& AN/ALQ-101(V) / RAF Coltishall

Opposite Jaguar GR 1A / No 16 (R) Sqn / 1 x 1,000 lb Paveway LGB, Phimat
& AN/ALQ-101(V) / RAF Lossiemouth

'Taking a look at the Jaguar, it can soon be seen that it is an aircraft designed for high-speed flight. It is small and streamlined, with a thin supersonic-type wing. In fact, the wing span is only 28 ft, has a low aspect ratio and is shoulder-mounted on the fuselage. These characteristics give the Jaguar a superbly stable ride at high speed and low-level, even in turbulent conditions.'

Flt Lt Andy Cubin, No 16 (R) Sqn

Above Harrier GR 7 / No 20 (R) Sqn / 4 x 1,000 lb GP / RAF Wittering

Opposite Jaguar GR 1B / No 6 Sqn / 1 x 1,000 lb GP, Phimat & AN/ALQ-101(V) / RAF Coltishall

'*I have always held the opinion that the Harrier is **the** jet to fly in the air force. When I went through training the Harrier GR 5 was then the "newest shiny" jet in the RAF, so I was desperate to fly it. When I finally made it onto the Harrier force, the aircraft totally fulfilled my expectations.*'

Flt Lt Bill Auckland, No 3 Sqn

'The difference between the Harrier GR 7 and the Tornado GR 1 is like chalk and cheese. Granted, you have not got the same warload or range in the former as you have with the latter jet, but from the standpoint of cockpit ergonomics, the GR 7 is far superior. Virtually everything is where you want it up front in the Harrier, with the only "cobbled on" bits being those added by British Aerospace in response to specifications from the RAF. The jet has got the performance and the avionics to do the job, is a nice platform to fly when bombed up and possesses a superbly airy cockpit which affords you a virtually unobstructed view in all directions.'

Flt Lt Nige Ingle, No 1 Sqn

Left Harrier GR 7 / No 20 (R) Sqn / RAF Wittering

Opposite Tornado GR 1B / No 12 Sqn / 2 x Sea Eagle, Sky Shadow & BOZ-107 / RAF Lossiemouth

Above Harrier GR 7 / No 1 Sqn / RAF Wittering

'Cockpit management in the Harrier GR 7 is a critical skill because the workload is very high for the solitary crewman who is perhaps diving on a target from high altitude, trying all the while to both keep the jet safe from attack and achieve a laser lock up for his precision-guided ordnance. There are a lot of things demanding the pilot's attention in the cockpit during this crucial phase of the sortie. Two TV displays and the HUD are all saying "Look at me" as you dive in on your bombing run, and a pilot must quickly learn to prioritise his time so as to ensure that the mission objective is safely met on a consistent basis. The single-seater still has a role to play in this high workload environment as long as the jet looks after you through the employment of effective cockpit ergonomics.'

Flt Lt Bill Auckland, No 3 Sqn

Left   Tornado GR 1B / No 12 Sqn / 2 x Sea Eagle, Sky Shadow & BOZ-107 / RAF Lossiemouth

Opposite   Harrier GR 7 / No 20 (R) Sqn / RAF Wittering

'The Jaguar has to be flown in a certain way so as not to exceed its limits – you can't just "roll and push" and take it for granted that the aircraft will remain in controlled flight. The jet is being kept well past its initial retirement date so as to allow the RAF to retain a cadre of pilots with sufficient single-seat experience to allow them to step straight into the Eurofighter sometime next century.'

Flt Lt Chris Hadlow, No 6 Sqn

Opposite Harrier GR 7 / No 20 (R) Sqn / RAF Wittering

Right Jaguar GR 1A / No 16 (R) Sqn / Phimat, AN/ALQ-101(V) & 1,000 lb Paveway LGB / RAF Lossiemouth

(Photo by Sgt Rick Brewell)

'The great appeal of the Harrier GR 7 is the challenge of single-seat operations. You have to do everything yourself. Fortunately, the jet is very much a pilot's aeroplane, for it handles even better than a Hawk.'

Flt Lt Bill Auckland, No 3 Sqn

Above Harrier GR 7 / Nos 3 & 4 Sqns / AIM-9L Acquisition Round / RAF Laarbruch

Opposite Harrier GR 7 / No 1 Sqn / 2 x SNEB, 2 x AIM-9L, 2 x 30 mm Aden cannon /
RAF Wittering

'It must be remembered that first and foremost, the Harrier is an air-to-ground weapons platform, and as such only requires a defensive air-to-air capability. Having said that, in one-v-one engagements the aircraft acquits itself very well, often holding its own against F-16/MiG-29 type aircraft. Its combination of small size, good manoeuvrability (rated to 7 G) and vectored thrust often surprises unwary air defenders.'

Sqn Ldr Rob Lea, No 20 (R) Sqn

Left   Harrier GR 7 / No 20 (R) Sqn / 1,000 lb GP & SNEB pods / RAF Wittering

Right   Tornado GR 1 / Nos 17, 9 & 31 Sqns / 2 x 1,000 Paveway II LGB, 8 x ALARM, Sky Shadow & BOZ-107 / RAF Brüggen

AIR DEFENCE / RECCE / TANKING & TRANSPORT

Panavia Tornado GR 1A

The Tornado GR 1A was designed to replace Jaguars and Canberras operating in the low-level tactical reconnaissance role, and were the first RAF reconnaissance aircraft to dispense with conventional 'wet-film' optical cameras, relying instead on an IR-based digital, filmless reconnaissance system, recording direct to video tape. This, the Tornado Infra Red Reconnaissance System, comprises three IR sensors with windows on the lower sides of the nose and a panoramic window below the nose, giving virtually horizon-to-horizon coverage.

The navigator can review and edit the back-up tapes from the sensors in the air, and no processing is necessary before the interpretation procedure begins on the ground, although the images on the tapes are digitised before the interpreters manipulate them. The IR-based sensors 'see' far more than a conventional camera, using a target's heat signature to provide a sophisticated image, which can, for example, differentiate between just landed and parked aircraft, aircraft with cold fuel in their tanks, and the shadow left behind after an aircraft has taxied away!

The reconnaissance system of the Tornado GR 1A is optimised for low-level tactical use, and for medium level reconnaissance, the aircraft can carry a Vinten GP1 pod, containing an F144 (Type 690) LOROP camera forward, with an 18-in (450-mm) focal length lens giving a 14° field of view. The pod's Tactical Stand-off lens/mirror assembly and rotating nose allows any depression, from horizon to horizon, and allows the camera to be 'aimed' by the pilot. Aft is a Type 900 A/B Panoramic magazine-loaded camera, with a 3-in lens giving horizon-to-horizon coverage. The panoramic camera can be used as a 'tracking camera' for the LOROP camera, and for plotting the location of LOROP images.

Installation of the new reconnaissance sensors necessitated the removal of the Tornado's internal cannon, but apart from that, the aircraft remains fully capable of fulfilling the basic Tornado GR 1's interdictor and strike roles, and

the two GR 1A squadrons (Nos 11 and 13, both based at RAF Marham) train in both roles, having a 20 per cent conventional attack commitment.

Reconnaissance Tornados upgraded as part of the ongoing Tornado mid life update will emerge as GR 4As, and these will be capable of carrying the RAPTOR (Reconnaissance Airborne Pod for Tornado) pod. This will carry digital electro-optical sensors operating in the visual and infra red spectrums and will incorporate a real-time data link. Among the sensors will be a long-range stand-off camera.

Above/Right Tornado GR 1A / No 13 Sqn / RAF Marham

(Photos by Sgt Rick Brewell)

BAe Hawk T 1A

Aproportion of the RAF's 99 in-service BAe Hawk trainers are designated as T 1As. Although these aircraft fulfil the same training and target facilities roles as the standard T 1s during peacetime, they are drawn from the 89 aircraft modified to be compatible with the AIM-9 Sidewinder missile – 72 of these were formally declared to NATO for wartime use, although this total dropped to 50 in 1993.

Although the BAe Hawk T 1A has no radar and no Beyond Visual Range missile, and is of limited performance, the aircraft's small size and agility make it a formidable opponent in a close-in dogfight. The RAF's Hawk T 1As have a vital war role as a point defence fighter, for which they would each carry an underfuselage 30 mm cannon and a pair of AIM-9 Sidewinder air-to-air missiles. Mixed fighter force tactics have been developed to allow the aircraft to operate effectively in conjunction with radar-equipped, long-range missile-armed Tornado F 3s.

Thus, in time of tension or war, the T 1A Hawks of No 4 FTS at RAF Valley and the Red Arrows at Cranwell could stop their training and display duties and would formally adopt their shadow squadron identities (Nos 19, 74 and 208). They would then operate as fighter squadrons in the point defence role, crewed by their instructors.

Right/Opposite Hawk T 1A / No 19 (R) Sqn / 2 x AIM-9L & 1 x 30 mm Aden cannon / RAF Valley

Boeing Sentry AEW 1

The Boeing E-3D Sentry replaced the ancient and primitive Shackleton AEW 1 during 1991, and marked a colossal improvement in AEW capability. The Sentry is a highly sophisticated airborne platform for the AN/APY-2 surveillance radar, with a slowly-rotating antenna above the fuselage. This radar is capable of providing early warning of inbound enemy aircraft, by extending radar coverage beyond the range of ground-based radars and of controlling and co-ordinating friendly fighters and ground attack aircraft. The raw data from the radar is augmented by inputs from the IFF and from the ESM system, the aircraft carrying 'Yellow Gate' ESM pods on each wingtip. The new aircraft's much improved performance allowed operating heights to rise from around 5,000 ft to a routine 30,000 ft, giving an enormous increase in radar horizon and thus range. Moreover, the Sentry introduced modern equipment, with longer range, greater resistance to jamming and better rejection of clutter.

The aircraft's capacious fuselage and more compact modern equipment also allowed the provision of more radar consoles and operators, enabling the aircraft to control more friendly aircraft, monitor more hostiles or unknowns, and manage larger, more busy areas of airspace. Datalinks (initially IJMS - Interim JTIDS Message Standard) allow data to be transferred to and from friendly fighters, ground-based radar and other friendly units, allowing the Sentry to co-ordinate the entire air battle if required.

The Sentry has a flight deck crew of four, consisting of pilot, co-pilot, flight engineer and navigator. The mission crew consists of another 13 operators, three of whom are classed as Airborne Technicians, wearing a unique AT brevet. The tactical director co-ordinates nine operators, whose duties alter according to the type of mission being flown. Two of the crew, the Communications Operator and Communications Technician manage the flow of information to and from the aircraft, using the datalinks.

The RAF's Sentries differ from USAF and NATO E-3s in being powered by the quieter and more fuel efficient CFM-56 turbofans. Uniquely among RAF aircraft, the Sentries are equipped for inflight refuelling using either probe-and-drogue or USAF-type flying boom methods – this makes them ideally suited for multi-national operations. The RAF's seven Sentries are operated by Nos 8 and 23 Squadrons at RAF Waddington, and have played a vital role in *Sky Monitor* and *Decisive Edge* operations in support of UN airspace monitoring operations over the former Yugoslavia.

Above/Opposite Sentry AEW 1 / No 8 Sqn / RAF Waddington

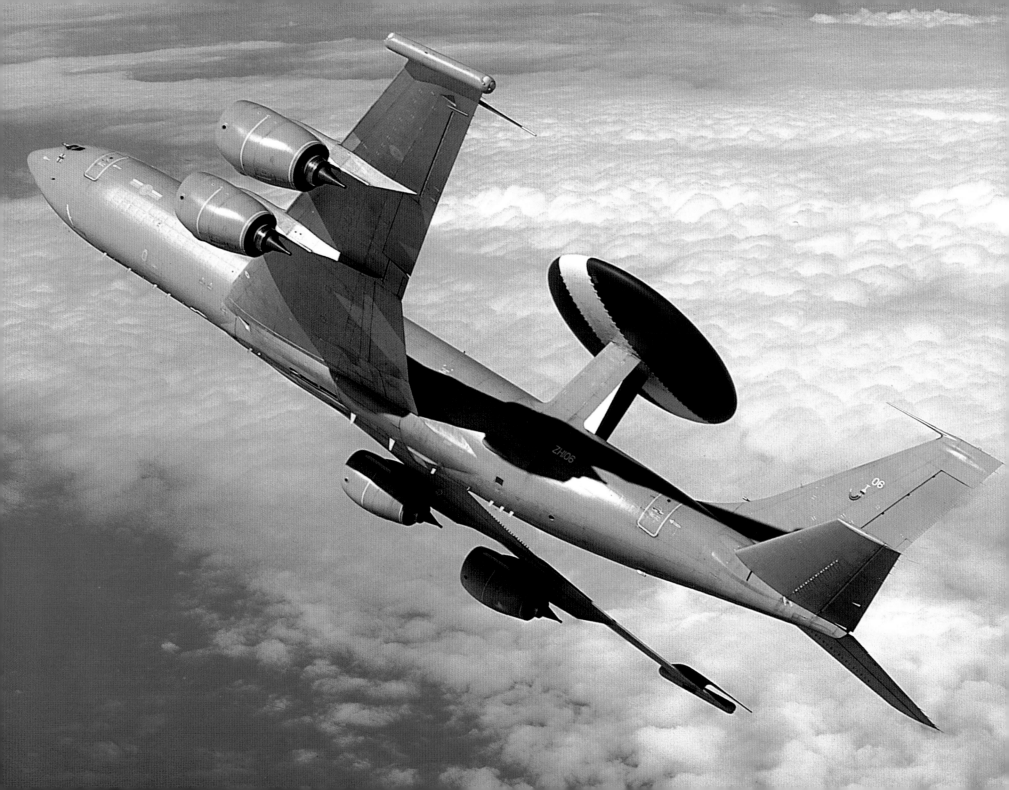

BAe Canberra PR 9

The Canberra first flew in 1949, and entered RAF service during 1951. Remarkably, a handful of these aircraft are continuing to provide an invaluable reconnaissance capability today, with No 39 (1 PRU) Squadron. The primary variant in use is the PR 9, with three aircraft officially on establishment, with two more serving as in-use reserves. Although the PR 9 is the youngest Canberra version, each of No 39 Squadron's aircraft is at least 36 years old!

Originally designed for high altitude strategic reconnaissance, the Canberra PR 9 has also fulfilled low-level and tactical reconnaissance duties during its long career. Today, though, the Canberra PR 9 no longer has a major frontline role, instead performing the vital survey and mapping roles.

Although no longer regarded as a frontline aircraft type, the Canberra PR 9 continues to have real operational applications, and is a vital asset to the RAF. Canberra PR 9s were deployed to Gioia del Colle for use during Operation *Hampden,* performing in the stand off (LOROP - Long-Range Oblique Photography) surveillance role. More recently, a Canberra PR 9 was deployed to Uganda where it undertook a major survey of Zaire and Rwanda, 'looking' for refugees. When operating close to a warzone, the Canberra PR 9 can now carry underwing BOZ chaff/flare dispenser pods on pylons only recently installed under the outer wing panels, similar to those seen on the B(I)8 and TT 18.

The Canberra's capacious fuselage can accommodate cameras and other sensors in seven positions. Today, a typical sensor fit might include forward and port and starboard oblique F95s in the nose, one oblique or two near-vertical F96s in the forward camera bay, an IRLS in the former flare bay, a Zeiss RMK looking through the new aperture in the rear hatch, and an automatic controller in the rear bay.

The Canberras are presently undergoing a further sensor and systems upgrade, which will apparently include the incorporation of a new EO-backed oblique camera (for high altitude LOROP work) based on the SYERS LOROP camera used by the U-2.

Two Canberra PR 7s are used by No 39 Squadron for high level radar calibration (UK radars reportedly being calibrated against the PR 7's radar signature) and these may carry wingtip chaff dispensers for exercise purposes, although they officially relinquished the target facilities role in 1996. The PR 7 is also used as a stepping-stone to the hot-rod PR 9 during pilot conversion, and can be used to save hours and landings on the mission aircraft during continuation training. Although designed as a reconnaissance version, No 39 Squadron's PR 7s do not undertake reconnaissance duties. The squadron also operates two T 4 dual control trainers, with another in long-term storage. The Canberra PR 9 has a provisional Out-of-Service Date of 2004, but its life may be extended further.

Above/Opposite Canberra PR 9 / No 39 Sqn / RAF Marham

BAe Nimrod R 1

Three Nimrods were delivered to No 51 Squadron in 1974 to replace Canberras and Comets previously used in the electronic intelligence gathering role. One of the aircraft was written off after it ditched following a major inflight fire, but this has been replaced by a converted maritime Nimrod MR 2.

The reconnaissance Nimrods differ from their maritime cousins in minor respects, lacking a MAD tailboom, and having a distinctive antenna fit on the nose and wing leading edge pods. The aircraft have undergone a number of improvement and modification programmes and are widely regarded as being extremely effective in their role.

No 51 Squadron's Nimrods have led extremely busy lives, and the squadron has played a vital, if largely unsung, role in most recent operations involving the RAF, including Operations *Granby* and *Corporate*.

The three Nimrod R 1s continue to operate in the reconnaissance role today, having moved from Wyton to their current base at Waddington during early 1995.

Above/Opposite Nimrod R 1 / No 51 Sqn / RAF Waddington   *(Photos by Sgt Rick Brewell)*

Vickers VC10 C 1, C 1K, K 2, 3 and 4

The VC10 is numerically the most important transport aircraft in the RAF inventory, after the C-130 Hercules. The RAF took delivery of its first VC10 C 1 in 1966, and since then the type has been used in the long-range strategic transport role, flying a mix of scheduled and special services, including VIP flights carrying members of the Royal Family and senior Government ministers. The aircraft was ideally suited to the military transport role, having been optimised for hot and high operation from third world airports, giving it very high performance and genuine global reach, albeit with a higher fuel-burn and cost per seat mile than some of its contemporaries. Carrying 118 troops and their equipment, the VC10 has a range of 4,900 miles even without inflight refuelling, which can extend the range further.

The RAF's VC10 C 1s are fitted with a large freight door in the forward fuselage, and feature a roller-conveyor system for rapid freight handling. For passenger flights, up to 126 seats are fitted, with up to 150 available in a high-density trooping layout. Mixed loads of passengers and freight can be carried, or mixed configurations of stretchers and seats. In the aeromedical evacuation role, up to 78 stretcher cases can be carried. Some 13 C 1s equip No 10 Squadron at RAF Brize Norton, a 14th aircraft having been scrapped after use as an engine testbed by Rolls-Royce.

Procurement of VC10 tankers was first considered during the late 1950s, but the availability of surplus V-bombers made such a step unnecessary. When it became clear that the RAF was short of tanker capacity, and when it appeared that the last of the V-bomber tankers were coming to the end of their useful lives, the RAF issued a requirement for a new tanker type. BAe met the requirement by converting nine ex-civilian VC10s and Super VC10s to tanker configuration from 1982. Five ex-Gulf Air VC10s became K 2s, while four former East African Airlines Super VC10s became VC10 K 3s. All were re-engined with Conway 550B engines like those used by the original RAF VC10 C 1. The aircraft also featured a large, five-cell fuel tank in the cabin, with

strengthened wings to allow the fitting of underwing Flight Refuelling Limited (FRL) HDUs, and with a third HDU and a rear-facing TV camera under the rear fuselage. A small passenger cabin was retained behind the flight deck to allow the carriage of groundcrew or supernumeraries, with up to 18 seats. The aircraft were also fitted with military avionics and communications equipment, and received nose-mounted inflight refuelling probes. The K 2s and K 3s equip No 101 Squadron at Brize Norton, where they were joined from 1993 by five K 4s. The latter were converted from ex-British Airways Super VC10s, part of a 14-strong fleet originally purchased for spares recovery and held in open storage at Abingdon for ten years.

The K 4 is a three-point tanker much like the K 3, although it has no additional fuel tankage in the cabin. The K 2s had such tanks installed by cutting a hole in the fuselage, while the installation of tanks in the K 3s was simpler, since the aircraft had large freight doors fitted. The ex-BA aircraft lacked freight doors, while cost and fatigue considerations ruled out cutting an aperture in their fuselages. Instead, the cabin can be configured to carry a full load of passengers.

From 1992, the C 1 transports of No 10 Squadron underwent a conversion programme to bring them to C 1(K) standards, with provision for underwing HDUs and a rear-facing TV camera, for use in the tanker role if required. The C 1(K) retains full passenger/freight carrying capabilities, and No 10 Squadron now operates in a dual tanker/transport role.

Opposite   VC10 K 3 / No 101 Sqn / RAF Brize Norton

The operation to recover the Falklands demonstrated the vital importance of inflight refuelling capability, and emphasised a shortfall in the RAF's strategic transport/airlift capability. One response to this realisation was the acquisition of six surplus ex-British Airways Lockheed TriStar 500s in 1983.

Two of the aircraft operate as K 1 tankers, with underfloor fuel tanks, twin FRL 17 HDUs underfuselage and a nose-mounted inflight refuelling probe. The new tanks contain 100,000 lb of fuel, raising the total to more than 300,000 lb. Although the aircraft are fitted with two HDUs, they function as single-point tankers, the second HDU acting as a spare, unable to be used at the same time as the first. Plans to fit underwing FRL 32B HDUs, making the aircraft three-point tankers, have apparently been abandoned. The remainder of the BA aircraft are similarly equipped for the tanker role (though inflight refuelling probes have been removed), but have also undergone further modifications by Marshall of Cambridge to become KC 1s. They have received a 140-in x 102-in cargo door, strengthened floors and a roller-conveyor freight handling system, and can carry mixed loads of passengers and freight while simultaneously operating in the inflight refuelling role. This makes the aircraft ideally suited for the support of deployments by tactical aircraft – carrying the necessary groundcrew and spares.

Three former Pan Am TriStar 500s were purchased in 1984, two entering service as pure C 2 passenger transports, with the third aircraft initially remaining in storage. The planned conversion of the latter aircraft to K 2 tanker configuration was abandoned, and it entered service, with avionics and other improvements, as the sole C 2A. The ex-Pan Am aircraft can carry up to 265 passengers over a range of more than 4,000 miles, but do not have inflight refuelling capability.

All of the RAF's TriStars, both tanker-transports and transports, are operated by No 216 Squadron at RAF Brize Norton. The squadron operates scheduled services to the Falklands and the USA, and regularly deploys tanker-configured aircraft in support of peace-keeping and ceasefire monitoring operations.

Above/Opposite TriStar KC 1 / No 216 Sqn / RAF Brize Norton

Lockheed Hercules C 1P and C 3P

The Hercules forms the backbone of the RAF's transport fleet, equipping four squadrons at RAF Lyneham. Two of these (Nos 24 and 30) are classed as route squadrons, while the others (Nos 47 and 70) are tactical squadrons. No 47 Squadron has a dedicated Special Forces Flight. Thirty of the RAF's Hercules C 1s were given a 15-ft fuselage stretch by Lockheed (the first prototype) and Marshall of Cambridge (the remaining 29) in the early 1980s to become C 3s. This modification raised troop capacity from 92 to 128, and gave a 37 per cent increase in cargo volume.

From 1982, the majority of the RAF's Hercules received inflight refuelling probes, becoming C 1Ps and C 3Ps. Other aircraft have been fitted with wingtip-mounted Orange Blossom ESM/ECM pods, AN/ALQ-157 IR jammers, and AN/APN-169B Station Keeping Equipment. Five tanker-configured Hercules C 1Ks (used primarily in the Falklands, by No 1312 Flight) have now been withdrawn from use.

Nos 24 and 70 Squadrons will replace their Hercules C 1s and C 3s with 25 new Hercules C 5s and C 4s which will be pooled for use by the squadrons, and as required by the OCU and OEU. The Hercules C 4 is the stretched version of the new-generation C-130J, while the RAF's last ten aircraft will have the standard length fuselage and will be designated as C 5s. The new variants will eventually receive an integrated defensive aids suite which will replace the mix of retrofitted chaff/flare dispensers, RWRs and IR jammers applied to the RAF's first generation Hercules.

First deliveries of Hercules C 4s were delayed by the discovery of minor problems in the aircraft's stalling characteristics, but Lyneham is now ready to begin taking the aircraft into service, with a new simulator and ground training building with equipment so advanced that a pilot could receive a CAA type rating on the aircraft without ever actually flying it! The RAF has no plans to exploit this capability, but training flying (especially in the circuit) will be much reduced.

Nos 30 and 47 Squadrons may re-equip with further C 4s and/or C 5s at a later date, or may receive the new European FLA (Future Large Aircraft).

Above Hercules C 3s / RAF Lyneham

Opposite Hercules C 3 / No 30 Sqn / RAF Lyneham

Panavia Tornado F3

The Tornado F3 is a dedicated, purpose-built air defence and interceptor fighter derived from the Tornado IDS which forms the backbone of the RAF's strike/attack force, with about 80 per cent airframe commonality. But the Tornado F3 is all fighter, with the performance, range, sensors and armament to fulfil the difficult role of defending the UK Air Defence region, and capable of fulfilling vital out-of-area air defence tasks.

The Tornado F3 today serves with six frontline squadrons (Nos 5 and 29 at Coningsby, Nos 11 and 25 at RAF Leeming, and Nos 43 and 111 at Leuchars, each with an establishment of 13 aircraft). Four more serve with No 1435 Flight at RAF Mount Pleasant in the Falklands, and 21 more with No 56 (Reserve) Squadron at Coningsby, the Tornado F3 conversion and training unit. Further RAF Tornado F3s rendered surplus by the end of the Cold War are earning their keep on lease to the Italian Air Force.

With its sparkling low to medium level performance and lethal mix of weapons (four BAe SkyFlash beyond visual range missiles, and up to four shorter-range heat-seeking AIM-9 Sidewinders), the Tornado ADV remains a highly effective intereceptor, and a difficult opponent to beat. With JTIDS and AWACS support, the Tornado crew have unrivalled situational awareness, and are able to use this to select appropriate tactics in order to defeat more agile or better-armed opponents. A range of modifications to the aircraft before and since the Gulf War have revolutionised the aircraft's defensive aids suite, dramatically improving survivability and adding to a long-running programme of improvements instituted soon after the type entered service.

The upgrade programme recently launched will further enhance the effectiveness of the Tornado F3, by improving cockpit displays, by making changes to the main computer and by allowing the aircraft to carry the AIM-120 AMRAAM and the short-range ASRAAM missiles. These improvements will allow the aircraft to remain viable well into the 21st Century, by which time the new European Fighter Aircraft will be established in service.

Above/Opposite Tornado F3 / No 56 (R) Sqn / RAF Coningsby

AIR DEFENCE / RECCE / TANKING & TRANSPORT

PORTFOLIO

'I've flown the Hawk against the Tornado GR 1 and F3, Harrier GR 7, Jaguar, F-16 and F/A-18. It will prove to be more than a handful for all of these types, and should prevail against anything without a radar. This is primarily because the Hawk is both small and agile, and when painted grey, the jet is virtually impossible to see when approaching head to head.'

Flt Lt Andy Gent , No 19 (R) Sqn

'The good thing about the Hawk is that there is nothing inside the aeroplane to worry about. You've got a compass, an ASI and a fuel and rpm gauge, and that really is about it! You can therefore concentrate totally on what is going on outside. Sat in the back of a Hawk, the visibility is better than when you are strapped into the front cockpit of a Tornado. It's fast, is great at aerobatics and extremely agile at low-level. It can also drop weapons which tend to go where you point the jet.'

Wg Cdr Ray Lock, Chief Instructor, RAF Valley

Left Hawk T 1A / No 100 Sqn / RAF Leeming

Opposite Tornado F3 / No 11 Sqn / 2 x Skyflash & 2 x AIM-9L / RAF Leeming

Above   Tornado F3 / No 11 Sqn / 2 x Skyflash & 2 x AIM-9L / RAF Leeming

Opposite   TriStar K 2 / No 216 Sqn / RAF Brize Norton / 2 x Tornado F3 / No 25 Sqn / RAF Leeming   *(Sgt Rick Brewell)*

'To survive in modern air combat, F3 crews have to be good at their job, no question. Self-discipline is everything – knowing when to press a good situation to achieve the kill, or recognising a bad one in time to get out and fight another day makes all the difference between squadron acceptance and credibility in peacetime, or life and death in war.'

Sqn Ldr Jon Hancock, No 56 (R) Sqn

'Having failed to make the grade for fast jet flying, I have been eternally grateful to those nav instructors who decided that I should be confined to the "Fat Albert" multi-crew environment. Not only I have enjoyed the globe trotting with like-minded, happy-go-lucky individuals, but I have also seen considerable and varied operational activity during 13 years of flying service. Those activities have ranged from tanker support for F4s intercepting Argentinian aircraft in the Falklands, to landing on dirt strips in Africa – not to mention three months in a tent in Saudi Arabia during Op Granby. Although there is the occasional early start and some unsociable flying to put up with in order to achieve the training and operational goals, life on a C-130 squadron can be both fun and rewarding. Detachments such as Red Flag have provided the opportunity to fly and mix with other NATO air forces, while support to famine relief operations in Africa and UN aid support to the people of the former Republic of Yugoslavia were possibly the most satisfying missions I have ever participated in. All in all, life on the "Herk" fleet is not only challenging at times, but also damned good fun.'

Sqn Ldr Dave Gunn, No 70 Sqn

Right   Hercules C3 / No 30 Sqn / RAF Lyneham

Opposite   Tornado F3s / No 56 (R) Sqn / RAF Coningsby

Above Tornado F3 / No 56 (R) Sqn / Sidewinder Acquisition Round / RAF Coningsby

Opposite Hawk T 1A / No 19 (R) Sqn / 2 x AIM-9L & 1 x 30 mm Aden cannon / RAF Valley

'Tanking normally takes place on pre-arranged towlines over the North Sea, although occasionally a request to "bootleg" a tanker can be made, to take on extra fuel if the tanker has spare give-away or a customer has failed to turn up. Tanking gives the force greatly increased flexibility, and is one aspect of modern airpower at which the RAF excels.'

Sqn Ldr Jon Hancock, No 56 (R) Sqn

Above   Tornado F3 / No 5 Sqn / RAF Coningsby

Opposite   VC10 / No 101 Sqn / RAF Brize Norton /

2 x Tornado F3 / Nos 43 & 111 Sqns / RAF Leuchars

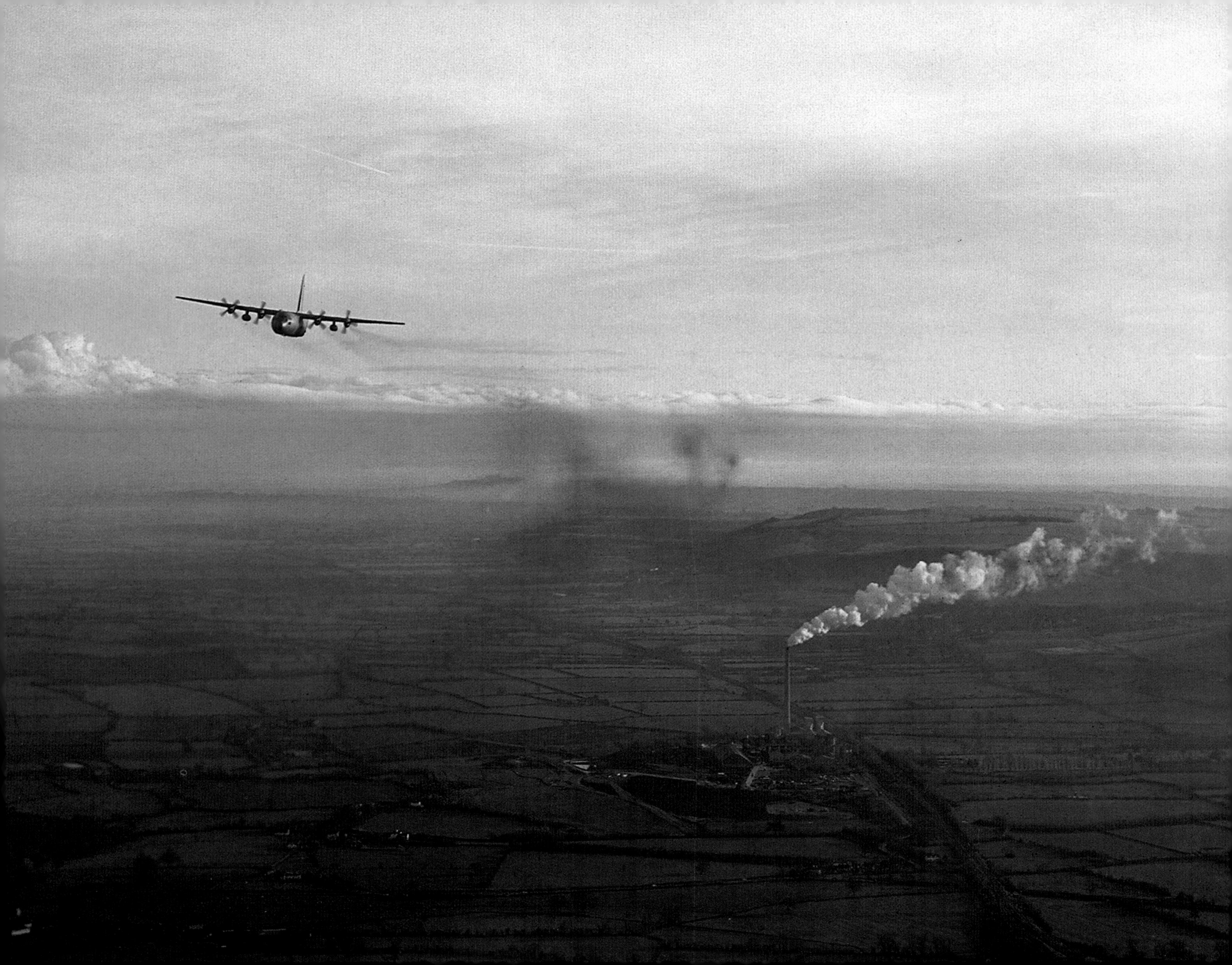

Above Tornado F3 / No 11 Sqn / 2 x Skyflash & 2 x AIM-9L / RAF Leeming

Opposite Hercules C3 / No 30 Sqn / RAF Lyneham

'The F3's turn of speed is very useful when operating as part of a large package that will see more capable fighters dealing with their opposite number, thus allowing you to sneak through and down your opponent's high value asset targets – maybe an AWACS or a tanker. When travelling at "Warp Factor Snot" it is very difficult for an opponent to engineer their missile intercept geometry on you.'

Flt Lt Steve Grant, No 5 Sqn

'There are some things that are just maddeningly frustrating about the F3. Flying on a counteroffensive air mission over Nevada in a Red Flag mission, restricted by the rules to fight in a height block more than 20,000 ft over the desert where every turn, every defensive manoeuvre, results in a net loss of energy. Despite the engines working in combat power, or max reheat, the energy curve spirals downwards into a bottomless pit, racing your stomach, waiting for the kill to be called against you. However, there are some things about the F3 that are just superb. Flying down low and as fast as your nerve and the engines will carry you, fighting on your terms as part of a four-ship where all the guys know and trust each other, entering a package of air-to-ground "mud-movers" with an advantage built on effective use of the radar and JTIDS, and where nobody, nobody, can run away from you.'

Sqn Ldr Jon Hancock, No 56 (R) Sqn

Left Tornado F3 / No 25 Sqn / 2 x Skyflash & 2 x AIM-9L / RAF Leeming

Opposite Tornado F3 / No 11 Sqn / 2 x Skyflash & 2 x AIM-9L / RAF Leeming

'The Canberra PR 9 is a very good aircraft, boasting power controls and two early Lightning engines which, although not making the aircraft appreciably faster than a standard bomber version, certainly allow it to climb at an impressive rate of knots. A great mount for the high level recce role despite its age, the PR 9 will prove difficult for the RAF to replace. Its systems have been progressively modernised over the years to allow it to keep functioning effectively in its role despite its advancing years. When you consider that less than two-dozen were built for use in this specialised mission tasking over 20 years ago, the RAF has certainly got full value out of the PR 9.'

Flt Lt Phil Flint, No 13 Sqn

Opposite Tornado F3 / No 43 Sqn / 2 x Skyflash & 2 x AIM-9L / RAF Leuchars

Right Canberra PR 9 / No 39 Sqn / RAF Marham

'Originally introduced as the MR 1, based on the historic Comet airliner, the Nimrod was uprated to MR 2 standard in the early 1980s. It is the first (and so far only) pure jet maritime recce aircraft type, and is in many ways ideal for the role, with its all important sensors having been progressively developed to exploit its capabilities to the full. High level/high speed cruise is performed at Mach 0.7, which allows all our distant targets or patrol areas to be reached quickly. Once on patrol at low-level, the Nimrod's agile handling at slow speeds enables ship or submarine targets to be prosecuted and attacked quickly and accurately. The responsive performance and benign handling qualities permits global operations worldwide from runways of 6,000 ft or more in length. A typical sortie will be of eight hours duration, extended if necessary by air-to-air refuelling.'

Flt Lt Sandy Barr, No 206 Sqn

'In a Hawk, what you are looking for in an engagement is to rapidly pile on in, get your kills and depart just as quickly. Once you are into a prolonged fight then you are trading kills with your adversaries.'

Flt Lt Andy Gent, No 19 (R) Sqn

Left Hawk T1A / No 19 (R) Sqn / 2 x AIM-9L & 1 x 30 mm Aden cannon / RAF Valley

Opposite Nimrod MR2 / No 206 Sqn / RAF Lossiemouth

'Trousers with expanding waistbands are the big thing for E-3D crews – with them being constantly bombarded with cups of tea, chocolate bars, curries and steamed puds! If you find yourself unable to eat another mouthful, the co-pilot will always help out – we are very big on CRM (Crew Resource Management) in that way. To be serious, I should mention the "kit", which really is magic, and is still evolving to full potential – the mission callsign of "Magic" is no accident. Certainly, the arrival of the E-3D into service gave a huge capability which the UK defence forces had not previously had, and it's now seen as a core asset for pretty much anything the RAF does, especially out of area. For its role, the E-3 is unquestionably the finest aircraft of its type in the world today, and ongoing upgrades should see it maintain that edge. The hi-tech kit is just one part, for the key element in the success of an E-3 mission is undoubtedly crew co-operation – with 17 of you, "it's good to talk".'

Sqn Ldr Kev Mason, No 8 Sqn

'Mental capacity is a big thing for an air defence pilot. You are constantly being bombarded with information from various sources, including GCI, AWACS and your wingman, and you may inadvertently miss something that your nav picks up. In a single-seat jet, this back up option is simply not there. A lot of trust and understanding is therefore built up between a two-man crew. This gets to the point where the pilot will instantaneously react to a navigator's commands in a combat situation without thinking twice about it.'

Flt Lt Steve Grant, No 5 Sqn

Opposite Sentry AEW 1 / No 8 Sqn / RAF Waddington

Right Tornado F3 / No 11 Sqn / 2 x Skyflash & 2 x AIM-9L / RAF Leeming

'The F3 epitomises the two-man crew concept of pilot and navigator, although the term "navigator" is something of a misnomer. Twin inertial navigation systems look after that department. Weapons System Operator or Radar Interception Officer would be more accurate. Whatever the name, if either crew members' performance is weak, the effectiveness of the F3 as a weapons system is severely degraded, such is its reliance on operator skills.'

Sqn Ldr Jon Hancock, No 56 (R) Sqn

Left   Canberra PR 9 / No 39 Sqn / RAF Marham

Opposite   Tornado F3 / No 11 Sqn / 2 x Skyflash & 2 x AIM-9L / RAF Leeming

'The VC10K is the last of the all-British built "big jets", and a true classic aircraft. In the tanker role with No 101 Sqn, it is probably the best AAR (Air-to-Air Refuelling) platform in the world. Without AAR the RAF could be limited to local defence of the British Isles, but with it, the force is a truly "global player". On task in the Gulf in radio silence, stacked with three USAF tankers within a few miles of the Iraqi border refuelling five Harrier GR 7s, and with eight F/A-18s joining you for more fuel, you know that this is what it's all about, and stuff that "truckie job" with Virgin!'

Flt Lt Gary Weightman, No 101 Sqn

Opposite VC10 K3 / No 101 Sqn / RAF Brize Norton

Right Canberra PR 9 / No 39 Sqn / RAF Marham

'Red Flag *in the "Herk" is a huge amount of fun and immensely professionally rewarding. To get the job done, you have to fly very low, and evade all of the "enemy" fighters and ground threats to get you to your target to deliver your load on time. You nearly always get "tapped" by a fighter either inbound to the target or on the way home. Fighter pilots who are not used to engaging a "Herk" at close quarters are always surprised by its incredible manoeuvrability. As a result, it's quite rare for a fighter to get a "kill" on a well flown "Herk". Throwing 70 tons of aeroplane around to ward off an "enemy" is the sport of kings.'*

Sqn Ldr Dave Fry, No 70 Sqn

Left Hercules C3 / No 30 Sqn / RAF Lyneham

Opposite Tornado F3 / No 25 Sqn / 2 x Skyflash & 2 x AIM-9L / RAF Leeming

'The Hawk will easily out-manoeuvre either Tornado type and the Jaguar – these jets rarely achieve anything higher than 5 G in combat when equipped with external stores, whereas the Hawk is quite happy "poling around" at up to 7 or 8 G with two Sidewinders fitted. At the type of high subsonic speeds we are talking about here, it does not suffer from a speed disadvantage over these aircraft either, despite them all having a reheat capability. However, the down side of the Hawk in this scenario is that the jet has no speed capability to allow it break off the engagement and "run away" – you either win or you get shot down, it is that simple.'

Flt Lt Andy Gent, No 19 (R) Sqn

Opposite Tornado F3 / No 56 (R) Sqn / RAF Coningsby

Right Hawk T1A / No 19 (R) Sqn / 2 x AIM-9L & 1 x 30 mm Aden cannon / RAF Valley

'When introduced into RAF service, the F3 had a formidable weapon fit comprising four Skyflash semi-active missiles, four Sidewinder AIM-9L heat-seeking missiles and a single 27 mm Mauser cannon. In those days, few aircraft had a superior BVR missile capability, and aircraft equipped with just heat-seeking missiles had to fight their way through the Fox 1 threat in order to get close enough to an F3 to employ their weapons. Sadly, the widespread introduction of the AIM-120 AMRAAM has changed all that, and now it seems that every "Johnny Foreigner" possesses at least the software required to fire them. It's a bit like going into a fight against a high-powered hunting rifle armed with just a cricket bat. Now, the brave F3 crew has to fight to get into an advantageous position to fire a Skyflash and then maintain radar guidance all the way to missile impact. Against a threat who can fire his AMRAAM and then run, it's just not a healthy option. That said, exposure to such scenarios has allowed the F3 force to develop some fairly effective anti-AMRAAM tactics, an aspect of modern air combat that other air forces are only just beginning to recognise.'

Sqn Ldr Jon Hancock, No 56 (R) Sqn

Opposite/Right Tornado F3 / No 56 (R) Sqn / RAF Coningsby

Above   Hercules C3 / No 30 Sqn / RAF Lyneham

Opposite   Tornado F3 / No 5 Sqn / 4 x Skyflash & 4 x AIM-9L / RAF Coningsby

'*You hit the merge with two great advantages – surprise and agility – and from then on in it's usually a short-lived encounter in which you should do quite well for yourself in a Hawk. This is essentially the form against a target with no AI (Air Intercept) radar and the same armament as a Hawk (two Sidewinders and a gun). Your skill as a pilot will allow you to prevail in this situation as long as your enemy decides not to "run away", as they can do 550 knots in this configuration, whereas a Hawk will only do 500 maximum. However, they seldom get the chance to break off the engagement on their own terms as they are rarely visual with you prior to the merge. Seeing that the Hawk is often used for point defence duties in any case, your target usually has to try and get through you in order to drop his bombs – thus leaving him without the option of "running away".*'

Flt Lt Andy Gent , No 19 (R) Sqn

Left   Hawk T1A / No 19 (R) Sqn / 2 x AIM-9L & 1 x 30 mm Aden cannon / RAF Valley

Opposite   Tornado F3 / No 11 Sqn / 2 x Skyflash & 2 x AIM-9L / RAF Leeming

HELICOPTERS & TRAINING

BAe Hawk T1

The BAe Hawk is an ideal advanced jet trainer, simulating many of the handling and performance characteristics to be found in the RAF's frontline fast jets. The aircraft is rugged and highly maintainable, with its thrifty Adour turbofan endowing the aircraft with remarkably low operating costs. The aircraft's long fatigue life will allow it to operate effectively to its planned Out-of-Service Date of 2008, and well beyond if necessary.

Intelligent planning of the syllabus allows cockpit workload to be progressively increased through the use of increasingly demanding sortie profiles. The aircraft is also a stable gun and weapons platform, allowing it to be used for the whole spectrum of advanced flying and tactics/weapons training, including operational tactics, air-to-air and air-to-ground firing, air combat, and low-level flying and tactical navigation.

In the weapons training role, the Hawk carries a 30 mm Aden cannon pod on the centreline, with practice bombs or rocket pods underwing.

Some of the RAF's Hawks have been modified to T1A standards (equipped to fire AIM-9 Sidewinder AAMs) to enable them to carry out a vital war role of air defence. The 'fighter' Hawk is described separately, although in peacetime the T1As serve alongside the 'vanilla' Hawk T1s with No 4 Flying Training School (Nos 19, 74 and 208 (Reserve) Squadrons).

Student pilots now remain with their squadron throughout a shorter flying training course which combines the formerly separate advanced and tactical phases. The latter used to be run by separate Tactical Weapons Units, under Strike Command auspices, and adoption of the new system has brought with it major cost savings. Proudly wearing his or her 'Wings', the RAF's young fast jet pilot goes directly from the Hawk to his or her frontline type for operational conversion, enviably well prepared to meet the challenges which lie ahead.

The Hawk also serves with the Central Flying School, including the Red Arrows aerobatic team. The aircraft is also used by No 100 Squadron at RAF Leeming in the target facilities role, and by the co-located Joint Forward Air Control Training and Standards Unit.

Above Hawk T1A / No 19 (R) Sqn / RAF Valley

Opposite Hawk T1A / No 19 (R) Sqn / RAF Valley

Shorts Tucano T1

The Tucano has now fully replaced the Jet Provost in the pilot and navigator training roles. Student pilot training began in December 1989. Although slower than the Jet Provost in terms of straight-line, straight and level absolute airspeed, the Tucano outperforms the older aircraft in almost every other area. The Tucano reaches 15,000 ft in half the time taken by the Jet Provost, for instance. Moreover the Tucano's stepped tandem cockpits provide a more realistic simulation of a 'fast jet' operating environment, and its handling characteristics are similar to those of the Hawk, with high rates of descent and deceleration made possible by the provision of a new ventral airbrake, and with single 'power lever' engine operation furthering the illusion of being in a jet-like cockpit.

The RAF's Tucanos are British-built (by Shorts of Belfast) and though based on the basic Brazilian-built Embraer EMB-312 Tucano, are considerably improved. The RAF Tucano's 1,100 shp Garrett TPE331 engine develops 50 per cent more power than the baseline aircraft's PT6, while fatigue life has been increased by 50 per cent to 12,000 flying hours. The new canopy is birdstrike resistant to at least 270-kt. The student and instructor sit on Martin-Baker ejection seats.

The Tucano is operated by the Central Flying School (for instructor training and standardisation) and by Nos 1 and 3 Flying Training Schools at Linton-on-Ouse and Cranwell for pilot's basic flying training. Pilots destined for 'Group 1' (fast jet) training fly 130 hours (147 hours for those on the long course) in the Tucano, the last 38 hours being structured as a lead-in to the Hawk. Pilots destined for multi-engine or rotary-wing training have a shorter course on the Tucano.

The type is also used by No 6 FTS at Finningley for training future fast-jet navigators, introducing them to a two-man crew, tandem seat cockpit environment before they progress to the BAe Hawk.

Above/Opposite Tucano T1 / No 1 FTS / RAF Linton-on-Ouse

Westland (Aérospatiale) Puma HC 1

The Puma has never fully replaced the Westland Wessex, though the two aircraft are of similar size and capacity. The Puma is considerably faster than the Wessex, and incorporates a number of features which make it more easily maintainable in the field, for example with engine cowlings which fold down to double as maintenance platforms. Since entering service in 1973, the Puma has undergone a number of modifications and improvements, with the addition of composite main rotor blades, Polyvalent particle separators in the intakes, and a comprehensive defensive suite. The rotor and intake improvements allowed a useful 600-kg increase in all up weight.

The Puma's defensive aids consist of door-mounted 7.62 mm GPMGs (usually one only, in the starboard door), with Marconi ARI 18228 radar warning receivers, AN/AAR-47 MAWS, Tracor M130 chaff/flare dispensers and an IR jammer. Pumas deployed to the Gulf during Operation *Granby* had NAVSTAR GPS linked to the latest Super-TANS 2 navigation system, and this formed the basis of the post Gulf War Puma Navigation Update programme applied to the entire fleet, with a new VOR, TACAN and ILS. The programme brought all RAF Pumas to a common standard, and included the incorporation of an NVG compatible cockpit.

The Puma has proved especially useful for supporting out-of-area contingency operations, since it is easily air transportable. The Wessex could be carried only by the long-retired Belfast (which could accommodate four Pumas or only two Wessexs!) whereas a Puma can be carried by a C-130 Hercules.

This capability has seen the Puma frequently deployed overseas, to Belize, Zimbabwe (monitoring that nation's first free elections) and Bosnia, while the aircraft was also used during Operation *Desert Storm*. Most recently, four Pumas deployed to Zaire for Operation *Determinant*, standing by to evacuate British nationals had such a course of action become necessary.

The Puma is primarily used in the Support Helicopter role, transporting troops or underslung loads of up to 5,500 lb. Soldiers can deplane extremely rapidly, using the aircraft's two sliding main cabin doors. The aircraft can also operate in the air ambulance role, carrying up to six stretchers and four attendants or 'walking wounded'. During peacetime, the RAF's Pumas are frequently used as air ambulances, and for the movement of kidney dialysis machines and other loads requested by the civil authorities.

A hydraulic winch can be fitted in the starboard door for the SAR role. The Puma may also fulfil a reconnaissance or surveillance role, with cameras or other sensors replacing the underslung load hook.

The Puma is expected to remain in service until 2010, principally with No 33 Squadron at RAF Benson, No 230 and No 72 Squadrons at Aldergrove in Northern Ireland.

Opposite Puma HC 1 & Chinook HC 2 / No 27 Sqn / RAF Odiham

Boeing Vertol Chinook HC 2

The RAF first ordered the Chinook in 1967, though the order was cancelled as an economy measure. An order was finally placed in 1978 and deliveries began in December 1980. The RAF's initial Chinook HC 1 was broadly comparable to the US Army's CH-47C, but incorporated some of the features of the Canadian Armed Forces' CH-147 subsequently adopted by the CH-47D. In service, RAF Chinooks were retrofitted with folding composite rotor blades and were re-engined with more powerful T55-L-712 engines.

The Chinook, as the RAF's most capable heavylift helicopter, was heavily tasked with the carriage of underslung loads, including ammunition, vehicles and fuel, but could also transport troops, as shown in the Falklands, where the one Chinook which escaped destruction aboard the *Atlantic Conveyor* played a pivotal role.

Chinooks played a vital role in the Gulf War, and subsequently in humanitarian relief operations in northern Iraq and Bosnia. Inevitably, the aircraft were fitted with various new items of equipment on a temporary, contingency basis, but much of this has been permanently integrated on the Chinook during the HC 2 modification programme.

Following the award of a contract in 1990, the RAF's Chinooks have been rotated through a rebuild programme at Boeing-Vertol's Philadelphia plant, emerging as HC 2s. The aircraft incorporate many new systems and equipment items, and with a 7,500 shp transmission. The aircraft's engines were upgraded separately (by RNAY Fleetlands) being modified to T55-L-712F standards with a new 'hot end' and a full authority digital engine control (FADEC) unit. This is estimated to give an astonishing 600% improvement in reliability and an engine life cycle-cost reduced by between 40 and 50%. The first HC 2 re-entered service in May 1993, and the last returned in 1995.

Externally the new variant differs from the original Chinook HC 1 in being painted in an overall dark green low infra red signature paint, in place of the old grey/green disruptive camouflage.

The new variant has a fully-integrated defensive aids system, with ARI 18228 RWRs, an AN/AAR-47 MAWS, an AN/ALQ-157 IR jammer, and M-206/M1 chaff/flare dispensers. Chinooks deployed to Bosnia received 250-kg of additional cockpit armour, mounts for three M60D machine-guns for the Gulf or two M130 Miniguns, secure UHF radios, Celton satellite communications equipment and had their RWRs upgraded to Sky Guardian standards.

In 1995, the MoD ordered a further batch of 17 Chinooks, three of them intended as attrition replacements, the rest forming part of the RAF's mixed buy of EH-101s and Chinooks to replace the Wessex and augment the existing Chinooks and Pumas.

Eight of the new-build Chinooks will be delivered as HC 3s, to a broadly similar standard to the US Army's Special Operations MH-47E, with plumbing for an inflight refuelling probe, perhaps with FLIR, and enhanced avionics.

The RAF's frontline Chinooks are operated by Nos 7, 18 and 27 Squadrons at RAF Odiham, and No 78 Squadron in the Falklands.

Opposite Chinook HC 2s / No 27 (R) Sqn / RAF Odiham

HELICOPTERS & TRAINING

PORTFOLIO

'The Tucano is a lovely aeroplane to fly, although initially it can be difficult to master because of the significant levels of torque response off the engine. The pilot therefore has to resort to diligent trimming in order to fly accurately, and the student's ability to master the engine torque, whilst simultaneously completing other sortie taskings, is used as a gauge by instructors to check if you have the capacity to complete the flying course.'

Flg Off James Morris, No 1 FTS

Left Tucano T1 / No 1 FTS / RAF Linton-on-Ouse

Opposite Chinook HC 1 / No 27 (R) Sqn / RAF Odiham

'The Puma is the "sports car" of the Support Helicopter Force. It forms an integral part of any airmobile attack, operating in a close battlefield environment, and it is a welcome sight to tired, wet and hungry soldiers. If you want to do a day's work take a Chinook, but if you want to have fun and do a day's work, take a Puma. From Caribbean Islands to the jungles of central Africa, from frozen Arctic wastelands to the Arabian desert, the Puma has nothing to prove in terms of capability. This flexible and agile battlefield support helicopter is favoured by both the aircrew and by the troops on the ground.'

Flt Lt A G Shenton, No 33 Sqn

'In a constantly changing military environment – both at home and overseas – our own forces, and indeed those of our allies, demand flexibility, speed and, most importantly, the ability to meet their combat requirements at short notice. There are a number of helicopters available on the market today offering elements of those features most favoured by ground forces. There are those which are bigger, faster, more economical and, ultimately, more aesthetically pleasing, but time and again it is the Puma of the Support Helicopter Force that is called upon to meet the demands of today's battlefield. Puma – "The Soldier's' choice".

Flt Sgt Simon 'OB' O'Brien, No 33 Sqn

Above Puma HC 1 / No 27 (R) Sqn / RAF Odiham

Opposite Hawk T1As / No 19 (R) Sqn / RAF Valley

'As anyone who has seen fog moving at 40 miles per hour, or sheets of the sea being torn from wave-tops and thrown at the coast, or rainfall so heavy and violent that it can flood whole valleys and wash away buildings, knows the worst of British weather can be a grim prospect. However, the Sea King can cope with all of this. With military satellite navigation, defibrillators, multi-band radios, stretchers, oxygen, anti-icing systems, equipment for cannulating and pain-relief, automatic search patterns in the navigation computer flown by the autopilot, signal flares, life-rafts and even a hot water boiler, the Sea King is well prepared to face any incident that RAF SAR can expect to encounter. Many people will be familiar with the sight of air ambulances and other small helicopters ferrying casualties around the local areas, but until they come across a Sea King, they cannot know the full capability of a rescue helicopter "on the job". Its two Rolls-Royce jet engines allow the helicopter to lift up to ten tons in weight, including a crew of four, half a ton of rescue and medical equipment, seats for up to 17 passengers and over three tons of fuel – the latter means we can remain airborne on task for nearly six hours, conferring a radius of action of approximately 320 miles, and still leaving us enough fuel to effect a rescue.'

Flt Lt 'Windy' Miller, 'B' Flight, No 22 Sqn

'The Hawk is a little sportscar. It's easy to fly, but is still fairly quick. The jet has responsive controls, and you can see out of it reasonably well. All these attributes, combined with the fact that it has no "fancy kit" in it at all – no fly-by-wire, auto stabs, weapons system or computerised navigation equipment – makes the Hawk an ideal teaching tool. It is simply a "stick and rudder" aeroplane.'

Flt Lt Bill Auckland, No 74 (R) Sqn

Above Hawk T1A / No 74 (R) Sqn / RAF Valley

Opposite Sea King HAR-3 / No 202 Sqn 'O' Flight / RAF Lossiemouth

ROLE DESCRIPTION

Offensive operations

Offensive operations are intended to destroy, disrupt or limit enemy operations. Counter air operations target enemy air power (preferably as close to its source as possible), attacking enemy airfields, and associated fuel, weapons and supply facilities, including enemy aircraft on the ground and in the air. Offensive air support operations may also be targeted against enemy ground forces. Attacks against enemy forces in contact with friendly troops, or in close proximity, are defined as Close Air Support missions, and may need to be closely co-ordinated with other friendly fire support, including artillery. Battlefield Air Interdiction missions are mounted against enemy forces immediately behind the FEBA, which are not yet being engaged by friendly ground forces. The Battlefield Air Interdiction role is particularly aimed at cutting off enemy forces in the battle area from their reinforcements.

When air attacks are mounted against enemy forces before they can be brought to bear, further behind the lines, they are referred to as interdiction missions. Operating beyond the range of friendly fire support, interdiction missions force the enemy to extend his air defence effort over a greater depth and are primarily aimed at the destruction of reinforcements and follow-on forces. Manned aircraft may operate against pre-planned targets, or may go out looking for targets of opportunity, effectively operating in the armed reconnaissance role. This is seldom a terribly effective use of resources. Attacks may be directed specifically against enemy air defences, in which case they are known as Suppression of Enemy Air Defence (SEAD) missions. SEAD operations can be co-ordinated with other offensive air support operations, and may even be mounted as direct escort missions alongside interdiction, BAI or CAS attacks. All air attacks mounted against enemy military forces, or against the enemy's direct military potential can be termed as being tactical, regardless of range.

Air power may also be used extremely effectively against strategic targets, aiming to destroy or disrupt an enemy's political, industrial and/or economic centres of power, thereby destroying his ability and inclination to fight. Air-to-ground attacks mounted using nuclear weapons will inevitably be strategic, since NATO and Western nations see nuclear weapons only as weapons of last resort. Their use can be authorised only at the highest political level, and not by a military commander in the field, and they convey political signals regardless of how they are targeted. A nuclear attack against enemy forces is actually a proxy attack on the enemy's political power, and is thereby strategic in character. Nuclear attacks by aircraft are referred to as Strike missions. Strike was a major role for RAF Tornados during the Cold War, but that role is now being relinquished and the Royal Navy's Trident-armed missile submarines will soon be Britain's only nuclear asset.

The RAF's current offensive aircraft types are the Panavia Tornado GR 1, the BAe Harrier GR 7 and the Jaguar GR 1A and GR 3. The RAF has four frontline Tornado strike/attack squadrons, all based at Brüggen in Germany (with two more at Marham operating in the reconnaissance and attack roles, and two at Lossiemouth operating in the anti-shipping, maritime and attack roles). One of the Brüggen squadrons specialises in the use of the TIALD laser designator, and two have a SEAD role, using the BAe ALARM missile. The RAF's three frontline Jaguar squadrons (one of which is partially tasked with the reconnaissance mission) are based at Coltishall, in Norfolk, but have an important role in reinforcing NATO's flanks, one being declared as a regional reinforcement squadron, the others to the Allied Command Europe Mobile Force. The frontline Harrier force of three squadrons is divided between Wittering and Laarbruch, in Germany.

Air Defence

The aim of air defence is to minimise the effectiveness of enemy air operations by minimising the damage inflicted by the enemy, while imposing the highest possible attrition on the attacking forces. These two interdependent aims ensure that as few enemy aircraft as possible are able to mount further attacks, causing less damage and interfering less with the defender's ability to mount operations in response.

The UK is fortunate in having one of the world's most modern integrated air defence systems. This consists of a highly developed command, control, communications and intelligence (C3I) system linking a modern detection system with the actual defensive weapons systems. In Britain, the C3I and detection systems are closely integrated within the IUKADGE/ICCS (Integrated UK Air Defence Ground Environment/Improved Communications and Control System) which links independent mobile radars with two Sector Operations Centres (at Buchan and Neatishead), and two secondary Sector Operations Centres (Boulmer and Ash, which is non-operational and used for training). These in turn are linked to the Air Defence Operations Centre at HQ RAF Strike Command (RAF High Wycombe), and to the Secondary ADOC at HQ No 11 Group, RAF Bentley Priory. These radars and control centres cover the UK Air Defence Region (most of NATO's Early Warning Area 12), some 750,000 sq miles stretching 1,100 miles from north to south, and covering most of the airspace between Iceland and Norway as well as Britain and its territorial waters. All elements of the IUKADGE are linked together by secure datalink (JTIDS – the Joint Tactical Information Distribution System) which also links in airborne E-3 Sentry AEW aircraft, suitably equipped Tornado F3s and Royal Navy ships. This allows an accurate, up-to-the-minute tactical situation to be built up and used by any 'link' in the chain. The RAF's Sentry AEW 1s provide a vital link in the UK's air defences, giving a useful over-the-horizon capability, and allowing radar coverage to be extended even during deployed operations. The aircraft are especially valuable in controlling and directing air defence fighter aircraft, but also have a role to play in offensive air operations.

Also linked into the IUKADGE is the Ballistic Missile Early Warning System radar at Fylingdales, whose primary task is to provide early warning of ballistic missile attack – an eventuality rendered significantly less likely by the end of the Cold War. Fylingdales is linked to similar stations at Clear (Alaska) and Thule (Greenland).

Insofar as weapons are concerned, the UK relies on a limited number of Surface-to-Air Missiles (SAMs) for short-range air defence (mainly Rapiers operated by the RAF Regiment). The longer range Bloodhound has now been retired, as have the Oerlikon cannon captured from Argentina during the Falklands War, and briefly operated by the RAF Regiment at Waddington.

The most versatile and flexible air defence asset available to the commanders of Britain's air defences are the RAF's six frontline squadrons of Tornado F3 fighters. These are based at Leuchars in Scotland, Leeming in North Yorkshire (both in what was the Northern QRA area) and at Coningsby in Lincolnshire (formerly in the Southern QRA area). Since 1992, however, only Leuchars has maintained a QRA (Quick Reaction Alert) commitment.

Manned fighters offer great flexibility, together with a 'man-in-the-loop'. They are extremely mobile, and can be spread out to cover a large area, or concentrated to counter saturation attacks by large numbers of enemy aircraft. The manned aircraft can be used to intercept incoming enemy aircraft, or can protect airspace (or project air power within a given area). Finally fighters can be used to provide defensive cover for friendly aircraft, escorting them on their missions. Offensive sweeps by fighters or escort missions more correctly come under the heading of counter air operations, and not air defence, though air defence fighters often perform these missions. The fighter can be 'scrambled' from alert status on the ground, or can be maintained at readiness in the air on combat air patrol (CAP). CAP endurance can be extended by use of inflight refuelling.

Reconnaissance

Reconnaissance was one of the first roles undertaken by military aircraft, and remains one of the most important. Reconnaissance is defined as the obtaining by visual, or other means, information about the activities and assets of an enemy, or concerning the characteristics of a particular area. Surveillance is closely related, and concerns the systematic observation of areas, people or objects. Reconnaissance and surveillance by manned aircraft forms only one element in the overall network of systems-gathering information, with airborne, space- and ground-based sensors combining provide the data necessary to plan and execute operations.

Reconnaissance has a vital role to play in peacetime as well as during war, deterring potential foes by demonstrating the potential to closely monitor their activities. Reconnaissance and surveillance can involve a wide variety of sensors; optical, electro-optical, infra red, and radar, and using equipment to passively monitor enemy electromagnetic emissions, including radio and radar.

Strategic reconnaissance operations collect the data necessary for the formulation of policy and plans at a national or multi-national level, while tactical reconnaissance provides the information required for the planning and conduct of combat operations. Target acquisition is defined as the detection, identification and location of targets in time and in sufficient detail to allow the effective employment of weapons.

Dedicated reconnaissance aircraft used by the RAF include two squadrons of Tornado GR 1As based at Marham, alongside a flight-strength unit of Canberras which operate primarily in the survey role. One of the RAF's Jaguar squadrons has a primary reconnaissance role, while Harriers deployed out-of-area can be equipped to perform limited tactical reconnaissance duties. The RAF also operates a trio of Nimrod R 1s in the reconnaissance role, these operating from RAF Waddington.

Modern technologies allow the transmission of reconnaissance imagery from an airborne platform back to a ground station in real time, and the RAF's

Tornado and Canberra reconnaissance aircraft will receive datalink equipment to allow them to do this in the near future.

Aircraft can play a crucial role in maritime operations, usually operating in conjunction with friendly naval forces, but sometimes autonomously, taking advantage of their greater reach and range. Maritime operations aim to contain enemy forces by inhibiting their forward deployment, aim to deploy defences in depth between the threat and its target, and aim to sieze and keep the initiative to prevent the enemy from mounting effective offensive operations in what is an extremely mobile and fluid environment. Air power has a crucial part to play in several aspects of maritime operations, including air defence and counter-air operations similar to the overland operations mounted by fighters and attack aircraft against land-based enemy aircraft. Two of the RAF's Tornado F3 squadrons retain a vital maritime air defence commitment, and the E-3D Sentries can also play a vital early warning and command and control function if required. But these are not dedicated solely to maritime operations and are described separately, under the air defence heading.

Aircraft are especially useful in the anti-submarine warfare (ASW) role, denying the enemy effective use of his submarine forces by overt or covert surveillance, and by attacking and destroying enemy submarines if required. Land-based RAF Nimrods can detect, locate, identify, track and engage an enemy submarine autonomously, or in conjunction with friendly ships, submarines and ship-based helicopters.

The RAF's Nimrods also have a role to play in the anti-surface vessel (ASV) role, searching for, locating and identifying enemy surface ships, shadowing them, and even engaging them with long-range missiles if required. The Nimrod can also control operations by surface ships, helicopters or other maritime strike/attack aircraft. The RAF has three frontline Nimrod squadrons, all based at RAF Kinloss in Scotland. Two of the RAF's Tornado squadrons (equipped with GR 1Bs and based at Lossiemouth in Scotland) have a primary maritime attack role, using the BAe Sea Eagle anti-ship missile.

Transport

The importance of the movement of men and cargo by air has steadily increased as out-of-area operations have assumed greater and greater importance in Britain's military commitments. The sensible use of air transport provides forces with a degree of mobility and flexibility that can sometimes compensate for lack of numerical strength. Though unable to carry the heaviest and bulkiest loads, transport aircraft provide reduced transit time, and allow the most rapid resupply of friendly forces.

Military air transport operations are categorised as being strategic (between theatres of operation) or tactical (within a theatre), and may be scheduled or reactive. Tactical air transport missions include airborne operations which move combat elements (and their logistics support and supplies) into an area, by parachute assault, helicopter assault or air landing. Special air operations may be undertaken in support of unconventional warfare, as well as clandestine, covert and special forces operations. Logistic support operations are concerned with the distribution of men and matériel within a theatre, excluding airborne operations, but including aeromedical evacuation flights.

Military air transport aircraft are not limited to operating in support of military operations. RAF Hercules, for example, played a crucial role in relieving the Ethiopian famine in 1984/5, delivering aid and improving Britain's political standing around the world.

The RAF's transport force includes four frontline Hercules tactical transport squadrons based at Lyneham, in Wiltshire, and a VIP transport unit at Northolt, in west London. Two squadrons at Brize Norton conduct both strategic transport and tanker operations, one equipped with TriStars and one with VC10s

Inflight refuelling

The use of dedicated 'tankers' to transfer fuel in flight to other aircraft can increase the range, payload, endurance (time-on-station) or flexibility of the receiver aircraft. The use of air-to-air refuelling can be of benefit to almost any suitably equipped aircraft in almost any role. Aircraft under threat of attack at their home airfield may be maintained in the air for survival, or to await delayed tasking, while combat aircraft waiting in the air can respond more quickly to short-notice tasking. Aircraft can be launched at lower fuel weights, insufficient for their planned mission, to take advantage of short-field take-off performance or in order to take-off with higher payloads.

Air-to-air refuelling is not a universal panacea, however. The process of inflight refuelling takes a relatively long time, during which both tanker and receiver aircraft are restricted in manoeuvrability (and are thus more vulnerable), while there is inevitably a limitation on the number of tanker aircraft available, and the amount of fuel which they can transfer. The importance of tankers makes them a tempting target for enemy aircraft, meaning that inflight refuelling almost inevitably has to take place in friendly, secure airspace.

The RAF was among the pioneers of inflight refuelling and initially used the technique to increase the range, endurance and flexibility of its nuclear-armed V-bombers, subsequently adapting the technique for use in support of air defence fighters, tactical aircraft, and eventually even maritime patrol and transport aircraft.

The RAF currently operates one squadron of dedicated VC10 tankers, with another VC10 squadron operating jointly in the air transport and tanker roles and with a squadron of TriStars operating in the tanker, transport and freighter roles. All Victor and Hercules tankers have now been retired.

The RAF's Buccaneers made use of the 'buddy' refuelling technique, in which one Buccaneer was configured as a tanker, carrying extra fuel and a podded inflight refuelling HDU (Hose Drum Unit). None of the RAF's current frontline fast jets are equipped for buddy-refuelling, though the option could easily be incorporated and has been considered for adoption by the Tornado, initially during the Gulf War, when a handful of aircraft were modified.

Support helicopters are used for the air transport of personnel and supplies, and can be used for the rapid movement of loads over difficult terrain. The cost and scarcity of the modern helicopter means that it is not simply a high-speed, all-terrain alternative to the truck or APC, however. The support helicopter role is thus more complex than might at first be imagined.

Although support helicopters can theoretically be used for the direct air-landing of troops in an air assault role, they are often better employed in providing logistics support, keeping just back from the frontline and transporting forward reinforcements and urgently needed supplies, including fuel and ammunition and specialist vehicles and weapons. Although a helicopter can be used to transport large numbers of main force troops, it is usually better to use support helicopters to transport reconnaissance teams, ATGM and SAM teams and other specialist troops, and support personnel and equipment in order to prepare for and allow a secure road move.

One of the most important roles for any support helicopter is the transport of underslung loads. This allows the carriage of loads too bulky (or too dangerous) to fit inside a helicopter cabin, and permits loading and unloading in the hover, without the helicopter having to land. The carriage of underslung loads increases drag and reduces range, placing restrictions on speed and manoeuvrability.

The importance of the support helicopter has been dramatically demonstrated in many post-Cold War operations, and the force has not been subject to the cuts which have affected other parts of the RAF. The heavylift Chinook serves with No 7 Squadron at Odiham and No 18 Squadron at Laarbruch in Germany, while smaller Pumas serve with No 33 Squadron at Benson and No 230 Squadron at Aldergrove in Northern Ireland. The ageing Wessex continues in use with No 72 Squadron at Aldergrove, and with the flight-strength No 84 Squadron in Cyprus, fulfilling a dual SAR/support helicopter commitment. No 78 Squadron in the Falklands operates a mix of Chinooks and SAR Sea Kings.

The versatility and utility of the helicopter is universally understood, but issues of limited availability, vulnerability, risk and prioritisation of tasks sometimes dictate a more selective use of the force.

During peacetime, support helicopters can fulfil a variety of national contingency roles, including the transport of winter foodstuffs when roads are impassable, flood and disaster relief at home and overseas, and aeromedical evacuation.

The RAF's Search and Rescue helicopter force consists of two squadrons (Nos 22 and 202) of Sea King HAR 3s and HAR 3As, operating as five detached flights around Britain's coastline. The units have a primary role of rescuing military aircrew who have ejected, but during peacetime spend most of their time rescuing civilians on the sea and in Britain's hills and mountains.

Training

The RAF still conducts the bulk of its own flying training, although increasing use is being made of civilian flying instructors and maintenance personnel at units as diverse as the University Air Squadrons and No 4 FTS. Some units are completely run by civilian contractors, including the Joint Elementary Flying Training School (JEFTS) at Barkston Heath and the new Tri-Service Defence Helicopter Flying School at Shawbury.

The flying training role encompasses the training of pilots, navigators, and other aircrew categories to operational standards, and is largely the responsibility of Personnel and Training Command, with Strike Command taking responsibility for operational conversion (type and role training on frontline aircraft types).

Pilots begin their flying training either with the JEFTS on the Slingsby Firefly, or with one of the University Air Squadrons on the Bulldog. All pilots then transition to the Tucano, 'Direct Entrants' at Linton-on-Ouse, graduates at Cranwell. Fast jet pilots undergo the longest course on the Tucano, before graduating to the Hawk, while pilots selected for multi-engined training go on to the Jetstream with No 6 FTS at Finningley, and helicopter pilots spend the shortest time on the Tucano before moving on to the Ecureuil and Bell 412 with the new contractorised Defence Helicopter Flying School at Shawbury.

Navigators do most of their training with No 6 FTS on the Dominie, Bulldog and Tucano, before helicopter navigators move to Shawbury and fast-jet navigators fly in the BAe Hawk at Finningley. Air Engineers, Air Electronics Operators and Air Loadmasters are also trained at No 6 FTS, principally on the Dominie.

Type and advanced role conversion is undertaken on the aircraft type which will be flown when the trainee reaches the frontline. The former Operational Conversion Units are now all designated as (Reserve) Squadrons and come under the auspices of Strike Command. Uniquely, aircrew for the Tornado GR 1, GR 1A and GR 1B undergo a two-stage conversion process, converting

to the aircraft with the TTTE at Cottesmore, before progressing to tactical weapons training with No 15 (Reserve) Squadron at Lossiemouth. Aircrew for the Tornado F3 go through a single-phase course with No 56 (Reserve) Squadron at Coningsby.

Harrier pilots convert to the aircraft with No 20 (Reserve) Squadron at Wittering, while pilots for the Jaguar undergo conversion with No 16 (Reserve) Squadron at Lossiemouth. Nimrod aircrew train with No 42 (Reserve) Squadron at Kinloss, Sentry aircrew with No 23 Squadron at Waddington, Hercules crews with No 57 (Reserve) Squadron at Lyneham, and other transport crews with No 55 (Reserve) Squadron at Brize Norton. The 'heavy' OCUs do not have their own aircraft allocated (though some station aircraft may wear the relevant insignia), and instead borrow aircraft as required from the relevant station 'pool' or from the frontline squadrons at Brize Norton. Support helicopter aircrew train with No 27 (Reserve) Squadron at Odiham (or on the Wessex squadrons), and the Search and Rescue Sea King crews train with the newly re-formed No 203 (Reserve) Squadron at St Mawgan.

THE ROYAL AIR FORCE

Principal flying squadrons/flights as of 1 April 1998

Strike/Attack

No 9 Sqn	13 Tornado GR 1	Brüggen
No 12 Sqn	13 Tornado GR 1/1B	Lossiemouth
No 14 Sqn	13 Tornado GR 1	Brüggen
No 17 Sqn	13 Tornado GR 1	Brüggen
No 31 Sqn	13 Tornado GR 1	Brüggen
No 617 Sqn	13 Tornado GR 1B	Lossiemouth

Offensive Support

No 1 Sqn	16 Harrier GR 7 and 1 T 10	Wittering
No 3 Sqn	16 Harrier GR 7 and 1 T 10	Laarbruch
No 4 Sqn	16 Harrier GR 7 and 1 T 10	Laarbruch
No 6 Sqn	13 Jaguar GR 1A/B and 1 T 2A	Coltishall
No 54 Sqn	14 Jaguar GR 1A/B and 1 T 2A	Coltishall

Air Defence

No 5 Sqn	13 Tornado F3	Coningsby
No 11 Sqn	13 Tornado F3	Leeming
No 25 Sqn	13 Tornado F3	Leeming
No 29 Sqn	13 Tornado F3	Coningsby
No 43 Sqn	13 Tornado F3	Leuchars
No 111 Sqn	13 Tornado F3	Leuchars
No 1435 Flt	4 Tornado F3	Mount Pleasant

Airborne Early Warning

No 8 Sqn	4 Sentry AEW 1	Waddington
No 23 Sqn (inc SOCU)	3 Sentry AEW 1	Waddington

Air Transport

No 24 Sqn	12 Hercules C 1 and C 3	Lyneham
No 30 Sqn	12 Hercules C 1 and C 3	Lyneham
No 32 (The Royal) Sqn	8 BAe 125 CC 3, 2 Twin Squirrel	Northolt
	3 BAe 146 CC 2, 2 Wessex HCC 4	
No 47 Sqn	13 Hercules C 1 and C 3	Lyneham
No 70 Sqn	12 Hercules C 1 and C 3	Lyneham

Support Helicopters

No 7 Sqn	19 Chinook HC 2/2A	Odiham/Aldergrove
No 18 Sqn	6 Chinook HC 2	Odiham
No 27 (R) Sqn	7 Chinook HC 2	Odiham
(+ Chinook conversion Flight)		
No 33 Sqn	17 Puma HC 1	Benson
(+ Puma conversion Flight)		
No 72 Sqn	15 Wessex HC 2 & 5 Puma HC 1	Aldergrove
No 78 Sqn	2 Chinook HC 2	Mount Pleasant
	& 2 Sea King HAR 3	
No 84 Sqn	5 Wessex HC 2	Akrotiri
No 230 Sqn	15 Puma HC 1	Aldergrove

Search and Rescue

No 22 Sqn HQ		Chivenor
A Flt	2 Sea King HAR 3A	Chivenor
B Flt	2 Sea King HAR 3A	Wattisham
C Flt	2 Sea King HAR 3A	Valley

No 202 Sqn HQ		Boulmer
A Flt	2 Sea King HAR 3	Boulmer
D Flt	2 Sea King HAR 3	Lossiemouth
E Flt	2 Sea King HAR 3	Leconfield

Maritime Patrol

No 120 Sqn	8 Nimrod MR 2	Kinloss
No 201 Sqn	8 Nimrod MR 2	Kinloss
No 206 Sqn	7 Nimrod MR 2	Kinloss

Reconnaissance

No 2 Sqn	13 Tornado GR 1/1A	Marham
No 13 Sqn	13 Tornado GR 1/1A	Marham
No 39 (No 1 PRU) Sqn	5 Canberra PR 9, 2 PR 7 and 2 T 4	Marham
No 41 Sqn	13 Jaguar GR 1A and 1 T 2A	Coltishall
No 51 Sqn	2 Nimrod R 1	Waddington

Air Transport/Tankers

No 10 Sqn	10 VC10 C 1K	Brize Norton
No 101 Sqn	14 VC10 K 2, K 3 and 1 K 4	Brize Norton
No 216 Sqn	9 TriStar K 1/KC 1 and C 2/2A	Brize Norton
No 1312 Flt	2 VC10 K 2, K 3 or K 4	Mount Pleasant

Target Facilities

No 100 Sqn	14 Hawk T 1/1A	Leeming
JFACTSU	2 Hawk T 1/1A	Leeming

(Joint Forward Air Control Training and Standards Unit)

Flying Training

Elementary

JEFTS	18 Firefly 11	Barkston Heath
(Joint Elementary Flying Training School)		
UAS	85 Bulldog T 1	Various
(University Air Squadron)		
VGS	Kestrel, Vigilant, Viking, Valiant	Various
(Volunteer Gliding School)		

Basic

No 1 FTS	66 Tucano T 1	Linton-on-Ouse
(including Central Topcliffe Flying School)		

Advanced

Defence Helicopter Flying School (DHFS)	25 Squirrel HT 1, 6 Griffin HT 1	Shawbury
No 19 (R) Sqn (No 4 FTS)	24 Hawk T 1/1A	Valley
No 60 (R) Sqn (DHFS)	3 Griffin HT 1	Shawbury/Valley
No 74 (R) Sqn (No 4 FTS)	24 Hawk T 1/1A	Valley
No 203 (R) Sqn (SKOCU)	3 Sea King HAR 3	St Mawgan
No 208 (R) Sqn (No 4 FTS)	24 Hawk T 1/1A	Valley
TTTE	16 Tornado GR 1	Cottesmore
(Tri-national Tornado Training Establishment)		

Operational Conversion

No 15 (R) Sqn (TWCU)	22 Tornado GR 1	Lossiemouth
No 16 (R) Sqn (JOCU)	10 Jaguar GR 1A and 8 T 2A	Lossiemouth
No 20 (R) Sqn (HOCU)	11 Harrier GR 7 and 7 T 10	Wittering
No 42 (R) Sqn (NOCU)	3 Nimrod MR 2	Kinloss
No 45 (R) Sqn (No 3 FTS/METS)	10 Jetstream T 1	Cranwell
No 55 (R) Sqn (No 3 FTS)	8 Dominie T 1(mod)	Cranwell
No 56 (R) Sqn (F 3 OCU)	21 Tornado F 3	Coningsby
No 57 (R) Sqn (HOCU)	6 Hercules C 1 and C 3	Lyneham

Glossary

AEO	Air Electronics Officer
ALARM	Air-Launched Anti-Radar Missile
AMF	Allied (Command Europe) Mobile Force
AMRAAM	Advanced Medium-Range Air-to-Air Missile
ASM	Air-to-Surface Missile
ASRAAM	Advanced Short-Range Air-to-Air Missile
ATM	Air Tasking Message
BAe	British Aerospace
BAI	Battlefield Air Interdiction
BVR	Beyond Visual Range
CAS	Close Air Support
CBLS	Carrier Bomb Light Store
DVI	Direct Voice Input
ECM	Electronic Countermeasure
EFIS	Electronic Flight Instrument System
ESM	Electronic Support Measures
EW	Electronic Warfare
FEBA	Forward Edge of Battle Area
FLIR	Forward-Looking Infra-Red
FTS	Flying Training School
GPMG	General-Purpose Machine-Gun
GPS	Global Positioning System
HDU	Hose-Drum Unit
HOTAS	Hands On Throttle And Stick
HUD	Head-Up Display
IFF	Identification Friend or Foe
IJMS	Interim JTIDS Message Standard
INS	Inertial Navigation System
IR	Infra-Red
IRLS	Infra-Red Line Scan
JTIDS	Joint Tactical Information Distribution System
LGB	Laser-Guided Bomb
LOROP	Long-Range Oblique Photography
MAD	Magnetic-Anomaly Detection
NVG	Night-Vision Goggles
RAPTOR	Reconnaissance Airborne Pod for Tornado
RWR	Radar Warning Receiver
SACEUR	Supreme Allied Commander, Europe
SAM	Surface-to-Air Missile
STF	Special Trials Fit
STOVL	Short Take-Off, Vertical Landing
TERPROM	Terrain Profile Matching
TIALD	Thermal Imaging And Laser Designator
TTTE	Trinational Tornado Training Establishment
VTOL	Vertical Take-Off and Landing